PRAISE FOR *EMPLOYEE EXPERIENCE STRATEGY*

D1570526

"Ben Whitter is not called Mr Employee Experience without good reason. He pioneered the concept. Employee experience, along with Amy Edmondson's related concept of psychological safety, may prove to be the most profound management idea of all. In *Employee Experience Strategy*, Whitter offers a blueprint for making employee experience a reality."
Des Dearlove, Co-founder, Thinkers50

"The workplace has changed radically in recent years and few people have thought about it as carefully as Ben Whitter. We've experienced the pandemic, remote working, 4-day weeks, quiet-quitting, social media boycotts, greenwashing, an office perks arms race and a new wave of Gen Z recruits arriving with a new set of expectations. Whitter is a savvy guide who navigates all these issues, through the lens of his Employee Experience philosophy."
Dougal Shaw, Author, *CEO Secrets*, Digital Business Reporter, BBC News

"Ben Whitter offers a powerful blend of inspiration and actionability, contributing to our quest for even more people-centricity."
Claude Rumpler, Chief People Experience Officer, L'Oréal

"EX has become the best retention policy around and a must for any organization. Ben Whitter developed the perfect blueprint to bring this idea to reality."
Dr. Ruth Gotian, Author, *The Success Factor*, Chief Learning Officer, faculty member in anesthesiology education, Weill Cornell Medicine

"Dive into the exceptional work of author Ben Whitter in his book *Employee Experience Strategy*. With his extensive knowledge and expertise in the field of employee experience, Whitter adeptly guides readers through proven and practical strategies. His insightful and expert approach provides the tools necessary to cultivate a workplace culture that fosters engagement and drives business success. Don't miss the opportunity to benefit from Ben Whitter's outstanding contribution and elevate your organization to new heights."
Marcelo Natalini, Dean, Latam Business School, Mexico

"Employee Experience is a very basic concept, intuitive to all of us who have experiences as employees, as customers, as people. But how do you take such a simple idea to a strategic level to the benefit of employees and companies alike? That is where this book comes in, with all its fresh insights, inconvenient truths, and aha-moments. Ben Whitter shows the way forward for HR and creates enthusiasm for the journey ahead."
Timothy Vermeir, Editor-in-Chief, HR Square

"Employee Experience can be a challenging concept to advance and implement in any organization. Ben Whitter has a gift for taking complexity and translating it into meaningful actions that any practitioner can follow. In *Employee Experience Strategy*, Whitter equips readers with thought provoking questions, necessary mindsets for change, and guidance to co-create an employee experience anchored in caring for employees and in business outcomes."
Christina Chateauvert Ph.D., Senior Manager of Employee Experience, Insurance Industry

"The profound impact of Whitter's work on my career and the affirmation it has provided for my decision to work in the field of employee experience, cannot be overstated. Whitter's remarkable ability to bridge the gap between theory and practice is evident in his comprehensive and insightful books, which offer easily adoptable strategies and real-life examples. I firmly believe that *Employee Experience Strategy* is indispensable reading for anyone aspiring to revolutionize their approach to employee experience and drive transformative change within their organization."
Julie Wix, Head of Staff Experience, University of Technology Sydney, Australia

"In the world of driving great employee experiences, we are competing with the best experience a consumer has ever had. We need a focus to make every day simple and special days really special. Ben Whitter does not only offer great examples and research but also clear strategic steps to deliver your compelling employee experience. I would highly recommend reading this book if you want to start or boost your journey on employee experience."
Tom Dewaele, Global Head of People Experience, Alphabet/Google

Employee Experience Strategy

*Design an effective EX strategy to improve
employee performance and drive business results*

Ben Whitter

KoganPage

First published in Great Britain and the United States in 2023 by Kogan Page Limited

2nd Floor, 45 Gee Street	8 W 38th Street, Suite 902	4737/23 Ansari Road
London	New York, NY 10018	Daryaganj
EC1V 3RS	USA	New Delhi 110002
United Kingdom		India

www.koganpage.com

Kogan Page books are printed on paper from sustainable forests.

ISBNs

Hardback	978 1 3986 0884 9
Paperback	978 1 3986 0882 5
Ebook	978 1 3986 0883 2

British Library Cataloguing-in-Publication Data

A CIP record for this book is available from the British Library.

Library of Congress Cataloging-in-Publication Data

Names: Whitter, Ben, author.
Title: Employee experience strategy : design an effective EX strategy to improve employee performance and drive business results / Ben Whitter.
Description: First edition. | London ; New York, NY : Kogan Page, 2023. | Includes bibliographical references and index. | Summary: "Designing and implementing an exceptional employee experience strategy is crucial for business success. From a leading figure in the EX field, this book provides everything needed to succeed.Employee Experience Strategy explains how to assess the needs of the organization and its employees, define and build an effective employee experience (EX) strategy and embed it successfully in the business. There is also guidance on how to get stakeholder buy-in from the rest of the business, and make sure that the EX strategy works for remote, hybrid and in-person working. It also covers how to overcome common challenges and measure the ROI of the strategy. Most importantly, this book shows how to ensure that the EX strategy delivers on the financial and performance goals of the business. This book is underpinned by primary data, research and global case studies from organizations including Microsoft, Google, GSK, Unilever, Tesco and Starbucks. There are also practical examples throughout and interviews with leading figures who have successfully implemented a robust employee experience strategy. Written by Ben Whitter who was recognized by Thinkers50 in 2021 specifically for his work in employee experience, this is an essential book for all senior talent professionals needing to build, embed and sustain an effective EX strategy"– Provided by publisher.
Identifiers: LCCN 2023021693 (print) | LCCN 2023021694 (ebook) | ISBN 9781398608825 (paperback) | ISBN 9781398608849 (hardback) | ISBN 9781398608832 (ebook)
Subjects: LCSH: Employee morale. | Employee motivation. | Personnel management. | Strategic planning.
Classification: LCC HF5549.5.M6 W453 2023 (print) | LCC HF5549.5.M6 (ebook) | DDC 658.3/14–dc23/eng/20230505
LC record available at https://lccn.loc.gov/2023021693
LC ebook record available at https://lccn.loc.gov/2023021694

Typeset by Integra Software Services, Pondicherry
Print production managed by Jellyfish
Printed and bound by CPI Group (UK) Ltd, Croydon CR0 4YY

This book is dedicated to Mum and Dad.

Always there; the first and most important supporters of my human experience.

CONTENTS

About the author xiii
Foreword xv
Acknowledgements xvii

01 The employee experience boom 1
The defining management idea of our times 1
Radical disruption of the HR model 3
Going deeper into the business 4
The great talent rotation 7
The EX technology gold rush continues 8
New workplace designs and new workplace practices 9

02 A new strategy for new challenges 15
Unravelling people strategy 16
Small moments, big impact 19
A world in financial crisis 20
Pain becomes power 21
Changed lives, changed workplaces 22
From culture to lived experience and performance 24
Life is the goal: do we really need purpose? 26

03 Co-creating the employee experience strategy 27
Co-creation first: everything else flows from there 28
Articulating what EX means to your organization 30
A high-quality start 31
Transforming with empathy 37

04 An ecosystem for employee experience success 41
An ecosystem to enable evolution 41
A universal approach to employee experience 42
Growing through strategic challenges 44
Conversations that matter 44

Deepening the holistic approach to employee experience 45
Employee experience strategy: a marathon delivered in sprints 48
Outcomes over opinions? 48
Where does EX strategy sit and who owns it? 50
What does EX mean to you (and those leading EX-impacting
    functions)? 52
Co-creation has already begun – building the blueprint for experience
    success 53

05 Experience masterplan 63
Experience masterplan – the ingredients of EX strategy 64

06 Team performance – a recipe for employee experience
    success 77
Experiencing team performance 77
Getting the philosophy right 79
A team approach – co-leading the employee experience strategy 80
Planning for high employee experience performance 81

07 Driving holistic employee experience performance 91
From awareness to performance 92
The Truth: towards a purposeful, mission-driven and values-centred
    employee experience 103

08 Reinventing leadership in the employee experience era 107
Alignment 109
Emerging leadership capabilities 110
Bad bosses derail the employee experience: great bosses elevate it 111
Core leadership capabilities for employee experience success 114

09 Aligning leaders to employee experience strategy 121
Leading the anywhere workplace 122
A connected workplace (and world) 123
Outcomes, outcomes, outcomes 125
The Make a Difference (MAD) milestones for managers 128
Certain leadership in uncertain times 133

10 **Playing to win with employee experience** 135

What does winning look like in EX strategy terms? 135
What are the factors that indicate a winning EX and company? 137
Imperfect actions, but positive progress 144
The strategic atmosphere around employee experience 145

11 **People experience: bringing beauty to the world** 149

Insights from the frontline of EX 149
Going deeper into the people and human experience 159

12 **Conclusion** 163

Answering strategic questions about ourselves 163
Brand leadership through EX 164
Challenging and co-creating with the status quo 165
Employee experience is a question of time 166
Every X matters 168
Strategic milestones, moments and momentum 168
Humanizing HR (and all support services) continues 169
Present moment performance 171
The AI-enabled employee experience is here 172
Driving strategic EX progress 173
We've only just begun 174

References 175
Index 181

ABOUT THE AUTHOR

Ben Whitter was recognized by Thinkers50 as one of the top management thinkers in the world for 2021 for his 'compelling' EX research. His previous books, *Human Experience at Work* (2021) and *Employee Experience* (second edition, 2022) were also published by Kogan Page. Ben is best known for pioneering and popularizing the concept of employee experience worldwide. He shares his work and research through his company, HEX Organization, the World Employee Experience Institute (WEEI), and via international partnerships that enable him to deliver his popular keynote speeches, strategic advisory services, executive coaching and the certified HEX Practitioner Programme.

His work has reached millions of business leaders worldwide, inspired the first EX conferences, and has been featured in publications and by organizations including *The Times*, the BBC, *The Telegraph*, *Forbes*, the *Financial Times*, *The Economist*, MIT Sloan, Thomson Reuters, *People Management* and HR publications globally. His acclaimed 2015 article, 'Bye, Bye HR', introduced employee experience to a global audience of one million. His content online and across publications is respected and recognized throughout the business world.

In 2021, Ben was formally named by HR Magazine as one of HR's Most Influential Thinkers, and he was also voted onto the list of top 30 global keynote speakers on the topic of organizational culture by Global Gurus.

Ben is a prolific global keynote speaker on human and employee experience topics and has introduced his ideas to audiences in more than 40 countries. His background as a multi-award-winning practitioner has created a strong foundation on which to build his research and ideas. Ben has lived and worked in eight countries including the UK, Australia, Italy, France and Japan, and for three years was the Director of Organizational Development at China's leading international university. As a result, Ben brings a deep global and local perspective to his work, which informs his approach as a frequent adviser, speaker and strategic coach to the world's top global companies. Ben supports organizations in the development of their holistic, human-centred and people-driven EX strategies.

In normal times, Ben spends most of his time between England, Wales, Europe and China; the world is his workplace.

You can work directly with him through HEX Organization, whose clients include companies such as L'Oréal, Sanofi, Unilever, Chevron, JP Morgan Chase, Suntory, GSK, Deutsche Telekom, and many more. Get support in developing your EX strategy by joining the HEX Nation at www.hexorganization.com

FOREWORD

Employee Experience (EX) is the simple idea that organizations can (and should) create a positive experience for their people. Why? Because it will make them more engaged with their work so that they do a better job. And when employees do a better job, customers get a better experience, which leads to organizational success. The underlying logic and business case is that people perform better when they feel valued and know they can make a positive contribution to something worthwhile. And thus, a virtuous cycle is created.

Some experts have claimed that customer experience (CX) is paramount but that is misleading. The causal link between CX and EX runs the other way. Ask yourself, do happy customers create happy employees? Or do happy employees create happy customers?

As deceptively simple as it sounds, then, employee experience, along with Amy Edmondson's related concept of psychological safety, may prove to be the most profound management idea of all. 'Profit is a by-product of work; happiness is its chief product.' So said Henry Ford, and old Henry had a point. Organizational happiness means happy employees, and happy employees make customers happy.

EX is also the ultimate talent magnet. Companies that fail to understand that won't attract the best people. It really is as simple as that. And yet, we know that survey after survey has shown that most employees are not engaged with their work.

In fact, research shows that if a company focuses primarily on profit maximization, it switches employees off. A 2009 Harvard study based on data gathered from 520 business organizations in 17 countries, many of them emerging markets, found that making the bottom line the top priority was counterproductive, with employees developing negative feelings towards the organization.[1]

Instead, CEOs who put stakeholders' interests ahead of profits generated greater workforce engagement – and thus delivered the superior financial results that they made a secondary goal.

The problem is that despite the overwhelming logic of EX, organizations around the world are still struggling to put it into practice. The reasons are threefold: first, despite protestations to the contrary, too many organizations *still* regard employees as disposable human resources – to be picked up when required and dropped at the first sign of economic trouble. And employees know it. Phenomena like the Great Resignation and Quiet Quitting happened for a reason: people don't feel valued at work. Period.

And the reason for that is because in many organizations they aren't! Hopefully, those organizations and the leaders who still don't get it will go the way of the dinosaurs. In fact, for all its negative effects, the pandemic may prove to be the meteorite that wipes them out.

Second, the advent of AI and other machine-learning technologies has encouraged some leaders to think that human beings and hence the employee experience will be less important in future. ChatGPT and its siblings do not ask for an experience at work (not yet anyway), they simply do what they have been programmed to do. But this is to miss the biggest change facing organizations today and in the future: that our humanity will be the defining factor in creating competitive advantage going forward.

Think about it. Putting employee experience at the heart of the organization is the most effective way to maximize performance. Even more so in a world where generative AI and other new technologies are removing all other points of difference.

Third, even the smart organizations that get the EX-point (a growing number by the way) do not have the strategies and tools to make it work. That's where this book comes in. Ben Whitter is not called Mr Employee Experience without good reason. He pioneered the concept. And the focus on the 'experience' of work as a management idea continues to grow. From transforming organizational cultures to HR's evolution into people operations, to the 4-day work week, to hybrid/remote organizations - all these ideas are based on improving the experience of work to deliver more sustainable (and profitable) people-centred businesses.

In *Employee Experience Strategy*, Whitter offers a blueprint for making employee experience a reality. He shows leaders how to build individual and organizational capabilities by approaching business and every other type of work in a holistic, human-centred, and experience-driven way.

Employee experience is a simple idea, but a challenging one to live up to. Organizations need strategies not just good intentions – and this book provides them in spades.

Des Dearlove
Co-founder of Thinkers50,
London, June 2023.

Note

1 'Why Profit Shouldn't Be Your Top Goal,' Nathan T. Washburn, *Harvard Business Review*, Dec 2009.

ACKNOWLEDGEMENTS

My sincere thanks to everyone involved in the creation of this book. Creating a book is a team game and I appreciate my family, friends, contributors and supporters who have helped make this possible.

As a coach to the world's leading EX professionals, I am profoundly humbled to be part of their inner circle advising, guiding and helping to shape strong EX strategies at companies worldwide. I find clients and students quickly become friends for life and I cheer their successes every day. Thank you for your friendship and trust.

My sincere appreciation goes to colleagues from Kogan Page once again who have helped bring this book to life. With three books now published, we really have created an experience universe together.

Finally, and most importantly, thank you to my readers for your vocal support worldwide and to all those leaders that are busy implementing the ideas I share within their organizations. My books to date have affected and influenced the lives and outcomes of many millions of workers and employees globally. I am very proud of that recognized impact and leaders should be very proud of their impact in EX too. It is a wonderful human-centred field and we are on the right side of history.

This book flows from *Employee Experience* (second edition, 2022) and *Human Experience at Work* (2021) and it has been a real-time collaboration with colleagues on the frontline of EX success. It is a privilege to share my thoughts, reflections and some challenges for your consideration once again through *Employee Experience Strategy*.

I thank you personally for joining us on this journey. Welcome, and enjoy the experience.

01

The employee experience boom

If you've been paying attention to the world's leading organizations in recent years, you won't fail to notice that something has been creating quite a stir within executive and management boardrooms. Not simply in one place, or one country, but in all places and all countries. Scarcely has a new management idea had such an impact on companies and how they do business, but employee experience has cut through the noise to take up a significant status and position within businesses across all sectors. Indeed, the words 'experience' and 'human' have never been talked about so much in relation to employees. It's an incredibly exciting time for leaders and professionals who are already engaged and ahead of the crowd in developing the employee experience (EX) strategies for their organizations.

The defining management idea of our times

Creating a positive experience for people in work is, as management ideas go, pretty simple and straightforward to understand. Perhaps this offers some insight as to why EX has been taken up at such scale and with such enthusiasm globally. It is easy to digest and comprehend, but, most importantly, to action at all levels of the company. It's as major as a huge investment in a global technology platform or a totally different operating model for work (hybrid, remote or in-person workplace), but equally it's as minor as bringing fruit, cake and a bit of humour to a usually dull team meeting.

Everyone can play a role in EX success at multiple different levels through direct actions. Some designed, some engineered and some totally organic within the workforce, actions on EX are not in short supply, but perhaps a unifying strategy behind them is. That's where a lot of organizations find themselves now – designing EX strategies that fit the times and fit some challenging new expectations on what work is and how it can be positively experienced to enable healthy business, and human, outcomes. It's an approach that is often positioned as the organization's response to a range of external and internal stimuli.

An antidote to the management challenges of the day

A lot of old ideas have been repackaged into copy and phenomena that gain traction and attention around the world. The great resignation, quiet quitting, rage applying and all the rest tell us something that we already know to be true. If employees don't have a positive EX, they will leave, disengage or even sabotage organizations from the inside. Any one of these trends across the economy can be traced directly back to the quality of the employee experience. We'll explore some of these newer (and older) challenges in the next chapter, but it would be good in the first instance to discuss where EX is and how far it has already come in its short life as a management idea that is being seriously applied in business.

EX has become so popular because, quite frankly, we don't get lost in strategy. We get immersed in actions; tangible actions that immediately improve things for people in their daily work or at certain milestones in their career journey. It's as wonderfully powerful as it is wonderfully simple to understand. This is one concept that may just avoid the management trap of becoming something that is too complicated, convoluted or abstract in the way we apply it into practice. Everything narrows down to the individual, the team, and the quality of the leadership and community around them. Increasingly, supported by data and its intelligent use, we can pinpoint precisely where actions need to be taken and this leads to rapid results and outcomes that no other approach can get close to.

An emergent global powerhouse of EX and people leaders

Taking forward this workplace revolution is a community of progressive people-centred and experience-driven leaders and strategists. From chief EX/people officers to EX business partners and EX managers, we finally have a group of people with the expertise to really take on the holistic people challenge. Without being saddled with the burdens of a more traditional and functional past, these leaders have thrown off the corporate shackles and begun to innovate and deliver outcomes across the EX. Commercial and brand leadership is a big part of what they do, yet they do it in a way that puts people right at the heart of the brand. Through this book, I'll share some of the insights that are coming through my work supporting, coaching and guiding EX leaders and their teams, and I am seeking to draw out some of the lessons that can be applied in your organization.

It comes at a timely point in the history of work too. The tension between employees and management has long been recognized, and despite the best efforts of HR, the trust gap is still far too wide for comfort. A massive round of strikes around the world offers some visible food for thought on this matter, but it is also worth noting the organizational response in general. The chief people officer (CPO) role is now one of the fastest growing roles in business based on the past five years (LinkedIn, 2023). Increasingly, this role is starting to actively reshuffle and upgrade the teams and colleagues around them into a more purposeful, people-centred and experience-driven future. This change is a long road though and this new generation of CPOs will need to prove and demonstrate the unequivocal value of EX to the business if they are to reverse the HR traditions of the past and the top-down approach of human capitalism.

In an ideal world, corporate structures would be filled with such colleagues, and with an eye on the future of work it is becoming more obvious that they will be in the not-so-distant reality of work. Just as organizations have elevated their customer experience (CX) leaders into positions of real power and influence, the same is happening with EX in real time. As one thing rises, other things must decline though to make space, and that's where things get really interesting.

Radical disruption of the HR model

Technology and more enlightened business practices continue to upend HR teams and structures as automation of HR tasks and administration creates space for HR teams to consider where they can make their biggest impact. Algorithmic HR will mean a lot more seamless experiences in work, yet that is not all of the answer for HR. Another part of that will be making some very tough choices about where to spend time and invest resources for maximum gain – this will come down to the humanization of the function, but how well the function can balance technology advances will be key to success. Employees continue to place a high emphasis on the human and personal touch. As HR evolves, so too must it think about how it rises to that human-centred challenge. Elevating the employee journey and EX is one such area that HR has leaned into in a big way. It is rare to encounter a HR function that does not have some foundational work already happening in relation to EX. New centres of EX are being created to encourage and grow EX capabilities across the entire employee journey.

The opportunity for HR continues to be centred around evolving into something that more closely resembles a people team for an organization, which aligns HR colleagues with the employee journey and EX. The danger that must be resolutely guarded against is that EX becomes too associated with HR from the outset and never has the opportunity to grow and become something that is truly led by the business. We'll come onto what that looks like and why it matters in the chapters to come, as driving a sustainable EX strategy involves many more functions and the business will need to determine which functions and colleagues are best placed to lead EX projects and programmes.

In that sense, EX is about curation, cultivation and activation. It requires a deep set of skills around collaboration and leading with and without authority to get things done. EX, for me certainly, is also a creative endeavour that harnesses and implements the best ideas from around the organization, so it's naturally very innovative and forward-thinking as an approach. It will change things about the organization's design, the roles and how they interact with each other across all support services, and how the organization approaches change and transformation generally.

Going deeper into the business

The starting position for EX is intriguing. Like most ideas, it begins life attached to one function or another, and either grows or does not. I suppose the big point of this whole book is to help it grow into a mature and multi-functional approach. It's such an incredible focus for businesses, we need to be aware of anything that stifles its adoption. This has been an impressive aspect of the rise of EX within companies worldwide; not only does it stay the course but it often changes into something much bolder as companies navigate their way into the field. Once a few initial projects have demonstrated the value of an EX approach, there is a definite spark and resolve to extend all of the practices and ideas across markets and territories. Then the question turns to scalability and the technology solutions that can help with that.

From mapping to strategizing, EX is maturing nicely as a strategic business approach. While there are many, many tools, techniques and methodologies that will support EX progress, the big one for me is getting the overall strategy right, and as we'll discuss in later chapters, crafting strategy is not done the way it used to be. I tend to work with the most senior of EX colleagues in my coaching practice, and I can consider them first and foremost to be, as you would suspect, strategists. Yet, I take the same view for more operational roles too. Each experience will require some form of strategy behind it if it is to deliver clear outcomes. Strategy involves some serious holistic and system-wide thinking to join things up and present a unified experience, and this is where practitioners are deepening their skills, capabilities and attitude. They are, indeed, becoming much more holistic in the way that they approach and practise their craft. Whereas in previous years I would certainly say this skill was lacking. Having experienced many companies working on EX, my position now is that it is a developing skill. People are paying attention to the nuances of their functions and how they connect to other functions that have a key impact on the employee journey. Colleagues are starting to network across the employee journey in real time to figure out where those major or marginal gains can be found to encourage all manner of outcomes, including:

- simplification
- well-being
- engagement
- satisfaction
- productivity
- reputation
- inclusion
- advocacy
- innovation
- performance
- belonging.

I'm not anywhere near tempted to put resilience on this list, as that word often raises its head in the midst of mass lay-offs and poorly executed leaving experiences. What it really means is how effective can the organization be in squeezing and burning out its workforce in the chase for profit – the term 'more with less' often comes up alongside it. Employees see right through that type of nonsense. By default, resilience is built into healthy and vibrant organizations that treat their people well and work to deliver positive experiences.

To achieve any of these things, or anything near national or world-class level, then companies have learnt by experience that they need all of their functions aligned, effective and moving forward as one. That is the best way to serve the business and employees, and it's great to see such solid progress in this regard. The days of being stifled in a narrow function with limited scope for cross-functional career mobility and collaborations are numbered. EX is creating a new breed of cross-functional business leader focused on outcomes, through deep work across the business working with all partners.

Belonging; here to stay

As a measure of a positive EX, there were some head turns in the early days when I used to talk about belonging as a core metric and outcome of EX performance. Do people feel like they belong? This is inclusion that is ramped up to create a real and healthy community. People can feel included, but it takes a whole different level of work to produce belonging as an outcome and it can't be faked. Companies need to do the hard yards to achieve the kind of workforce where that sense of belonging is high. Thankfully, the power of belonging has ensured businesses are paying much more attention to this within their diversity, inclusion and equality programmes.

Indeed, belonging is often a core and stated objective and theme within EX strategies and long may it continue. The rise of EX and belonging as a management focus can be tied together, and the only question is how far companies can go with this – it is no longer adequate to create a sense of belonging that revolves around a company's HQ or a regional office. In this changed world of work, EX leaders are getting creative about how they scale belonging across countries and regions, but also towns and cities given that a proportion of the global workforce continues to enjoy home and remote working. Another aspect within this theme of EX is the contingent, contractual and alternative workforce. How do you build belonging into the company given these sometimes wildly different populations with their very different expectations? This is what I consider the rarely explored frontier of EX where we operate sometimes in the grey areas of employment and contractual relationships. In saying this, a sensible EX strategy will consider all groups of workers and will scale and develop experiences accordingly to suit different types of workers.

The great talent rotation

A common theme has emerged in my work on EX over the years and it is worth noting from the outset of this book. I started my (first) career on the frontline of sales and customer service. It was those early roles that fundamentally shaped my early views about what businesses are there to do. They are in business to be of value and to serve. That is it. There's nothing much else beyond this because if they do those things very well, profit, money and growth tend to come. If they don't do those things, then progress will be severely limited. Now, it is employees and workers that serve and deliver that value in practice.

My view then when I entered my HR career was that these simple truths would be reflected in the way HR does its work and the way it thinks about employees. Well, I was totally wrong. People and their experiences were as far from the HR radar as you can get. I was pretty shocked about that at the time as I would have expected swift and complete actions to help the organization's value creators wherever they were. I have to say though, I'm far from alone. EX attracts business and commercial leaders. Indeed, some of the best performing EX leaders have had varied career experiences away from the traditional or associated HR functions. This gives them a different view and they get to work on different problems. More importantly, they see and experience the organization differently. Their work reflects this as does their ambition for the EX strategy and its constituent parts.

For these reasons, we need to continue to extend the EX talent pool while ensuring leaders in more traditional employee-facing roles get to work with and experience commercial roles directly in some form. Companies must ensure that employees in key support roles experience the frontlines of their business. This leads to such a profound mindset shift that it will literally save companies from spending fortunes on leadership workshops and the like that rarely make the difference they set out to. It also leads to better products, better services and better outcomes for employees. It's a massive win to rotate talent into and around EX roles and it will contribute greatly to elevating the status of EX within a business.

The EX technology gold rush continues

EX is in its boom era, for sure. With new start-ups, established powerhouses, new platforms and new products coming to the market all the time, EX is now viewed as the anchor of a major organizational ecosystem of services that support and enable employees. It is unusual to see vendors not talking about EX if they are operating anywhere close to the employee services space. The sales and PR spin surrounding EX has ramped up noticeably during and beyond the pandemic. Still, positioning and connecting such vendors with an audience remains complicated given that EX may be positioned across functions or across specialisms. The more bespoke products and services, say for hiring and onboarding practices, can often experience many hurdles in securing clients – the organization and the accountabilities for EX is a mixed picture of responsibilities. The contacts that these vendors look for and cultivate relationships with may not necessarily be the EX decision maker overall.

From the commissioner perspective, it will take a keen eye to really recognize the true EX innovators out of those that have simply re-marketed existing engagement, well-being, productivity or communication products, but it's not that difficult if the market is being continually explored for the latest technology that can enhance the EX. Simplification of processes has been a real winner here, as new technology has often been the catalyst for a deep dive into all kinds of processes that may be frustrating or adding to a complexity that doesn't really need to exist within the organization. EX is data hungry and again, big winners in the EX technology space are vendors with platforms that can harness and harvest a treasure trove of actionable data to inform and improve the employee journey, and EX overall. Augmented listening tools and software, and platforms that bring everything together from the employee's perspective – their digital work life and EX in one place – is also in the ascendency, with a big push in the market by significant global players. No one has quite reached the EX utopia that emerging technology promises, yet it is still a positive development that employees are experiencing higher quality digital experiences. Clearly, decisions here will need to be astute and take place in the context of what the organization has already invested in and the future state it wants to create, but simplification remains high on the agenda within EX efforts.

New workplace designs and new workplace practices

No doubt the heat map of activity on the EX map will be based around the actual workplace, physical, virtual, or bits of both. This, of course, dominated executive conversations during and immediately following the pandemic, with shifts taking place in a variety of directions, with a lot of debate alongside it. There are now work models in play that employees have been actively railing against. It's an unusual situation really. Employees have been nothing but consistent on this issue and take every opportunity to reinforce their position, which is namely that they want more choice, control and flexibility in their careers. This is a delicate balancing act for EX leaders and CPOs, but let's face it, the decision may be well out of their hands. There's been a lot of swashbuckling CEO behaviour on this issue, with CEOs actively leading the return to the office or the pro-remote work communication campaigns. It will come down to a personal point of view in many instances. Interestingly, there does seem to be a lot of ideology rather than evidence floating about these days when it comes to the optimum workplace. Certainly, those claiming to be employee-centred while actively working against the direct wishes of their talented workforces may come unstuck later down the line based on the choices of their top teams.

Several of my clients have taken the opportunity to upgrade their real estate and campuses to ensure they are high impact social places where natural collaboration and connection can create positive relationships. There's also a lot more focus on well-being within the physical estate and ensuring employees have the spaces they need to suit their different work styles and modes. Others have opted to sell the lot off and stay online, and rent venues as and when needed for high value social events, gatherings and team meetings.

Who is right? I don't lean one way or the other on this – I lean into the context of the company, as that's where leaders should be focused, not on what everyone else is doing. What's right for one company will be a disaster for another so contextual intelligence is going to need to be in high supply across EX roles to make a success out of whatever work models companies opt for. The same applies for the novelty that is the four-day week, which has proven to be successful in many contexts now. I wonder why. It's probably because employees get a day back to do as they please or have more control over the most important aspect of life – time. Do you know what's even better than the four-day week? A three-day week, or even a one-day week. The part-time workforce has exploded.

Indeed, upwards of 8 million people – a quarter of the total UK work-force – is now made up of part-time workers, according to the Office for National Statistics (ONS). This figure is representative of the connection between companies, society and national policy, and its impact on the EX. If the cost of a commute is too high, the cost of childcare is too high or work–life balance suffers, there might well be far too few incentives to take on more hours or become a full-time worker again. Employers will feel the impact of this, of course, and it will determine the kind of workforce that they have in the future and on what terms. Is it not a state of ridiculousness that a full-time worker can often end up taking home less money than if they worked part-time hours? Employees are doing the maths for themselves and choosing accordingly based on their own costs or lifestyles.

The same goes for the retiree population who are opting in high numbers to finish their careers early and do their own thing. Successive governments have primed these conditions and the unintended consequences are unfold-ing over recent years to stifle growth and productivity across developed economies. This will be a factor and will need some serious care and atten-tion when looking at the EX strategy and the demographics (and desires) of the workforce. At the top of that priority shopping list from employees is well-being outcomes.

Well-being surges onto the EX radar

If we're looking at the EX, we're looking at people, and there are not many things being talked about with more intensity than the well-being of an organization's people. It was an emerging priority within EX prior to the pandemic, but clearly, things have accelerated since. There is a greater awareness and sophistication to well-being efforts, and it is seen as a corpo-rate priority to have a healthy organization. This has taken shape in various forms across the employee journey – driven by people and technology – and companies are being more careful to weave well-being into the organization rather than position it as something that stands alone and outside of the mainstream EX. Indeed, well-being has become an outcome of a positive EX and is talked about in those terms on a more consistent basis.

Employee well-being focuses on the mental, physical, emotional and economic health of employees, and is very aligned to the holistic nature of EX as I've presented it. We need to look at the organization holistically and we also need to consider the human being in a holistic way too – how deci-sions are made, how people are treated during HR processes, what support and tools are in place to support health outcomes. On the organization side, we talk about engagement as one major outcome of EX. On the individual side, we talk about well-being as a major outcome. In reality, both the employee and employer benefit from both outcomes, and they are very closely aligned. This is why well-being now features heavily in slide decks and business cases about the merits and outcomes associated with EX.

The voice of the employee gets even louder

A growing unrest following a global pandemic was always going to present itself given the amount and scale of issues that the world's employees have had to endure over the last few years. The voice of the employee was getting louder even before the pandemic, with many more ways to share dissatisfaction with an employer, and many more ways (and options) to take action about it. Campus activism and strikes are happening now with alarming regularity. It's amazing to give employees platforms and surveys so that they can share their views, concerns and also vent their frustration, but what if no one listens? Or worse still, what if company leaders don't care? It's a recipe for long-term discontent.

Interestingly, I have been engaged to deliver workshops and speeches a number of times in different parts of the world where, coincidentally, major industrial action was taking place on the very day of my visit. While I enjoyed the irony of being booked to talk about employee experience in the midst of major and chaotic strike action, I must say that these are not experiences I wish to repeat. It is my sincere hope that we learn the lessons of employee experience and find much better ways to restore or even build trust across workplaces. Whether it is the unions, employees or companies themselves, it is not in anyone's interest to engage in these 'them and us' battles that get completely out of hand and end up trashing the organization entirely. We'll look at how we can start to do this, but back and forth consultation and politics is not going to solve these challenges. We need a better approach altogether to make progress.

In EX strategy terms then, there are some serious ramifications. We can't just use the tired consult and comply model to bring projects to fruition; it just doesn't work. It is the method that continues to be rolled out in companies today by default, but that doesn't necessarily mean it's the right approach, especially when working on EX projects which demand a much higher level of involvement and engagement from employees.

SUMMARY

There's a lot of excellent progress in the field as capabilities and teams grow, and companies are positioning themselves strongly to perform to high standards across the entire employee journey from pre-hire to retire. A few things are no longer in any doubt:

- EX is in the ascendancy within organizations as a topic of focus, debate and action.

- Organizations are approaching the topic with much more thought, rigour and intelligence.

- Execution is starting to catch up with intention as companies start building EX strategies that will unlock the great potential of their employees and the organization.

- EX is now an essential item of the strategic business discussion across senior management circles and, as a concept, it is starting to break through into all levels of management.

- Business models are under pressure from all stakeholders to incorporate, integrate and improve EX performance.

- Employees have welcomed and endorsed EX as a strategic and operational approach. Focusing on experiences, human centricity and co-creation are recognized behaviours of the world's most trusted and admired brands.

It's exceptionally difficult to argue with anyone who wants to improve our experiences and outcomes in life. I suppose that's the beauty of the strategic business case for EX – employees are all for it, and executives are realizing en-masse how the EX shapes and directs overall business performance and that all-important connection with their employees and workers. Still, EX strategy takes things to the next level in driving alignment and outcomes. It creates connections between projects, programmes and work that touch the EX.

Indeed, anything that affects the EX is in play and is part of the strategic picture. Whether short, medium or long term, businesses are getting much better at seeing the EX for what it is and how everything – every interaction, every moment, every decision, every policy, every practice and every experience – comes together holistically to define an organization in and beyond the marketplace. While EX has been gathering pace for several years, good EX strategy has been lagging well behind. A few projects or technologies here and there labelled up as EX is not the EX I recognize. The EX that I've tried to advance in the global economy is one that is whole, connected and unified. To that end, this book will share a number of insights from my work about how companies are approaching EX in a more complete and holistic way at a strategic level.

There are always a lot of trends occurring at any given time within an organization and the people profession. Employers place their bets on the latest technology or management idea; yet no matter where I look, EX has become synonymous with brand progress and it is now ever-present on the agendas of all employee-facing leaders. Why is that? Well, it's booming because we always have a choice – we can always do something positive in EX at any given moment or through any given challenge; we can always make something better. EX is the ultimate management idea and has proven to be consistently actionable with verifiable results never far away. It is not abstract, it is tangible, and businesses (and people) enjoy that very much. The EX profession as a whole, and throughout all those roles that connect and contribute to it, is prime time within business. We now need to maximize all of our strategic opportunities to deliver positive business-growing employee experiences, and all the great business results that they bring. The employee experience is the defining challenge and opportunity for organizations of today, and a strong EX strategy is the foundation stone in building genuine and long-lasting business success.

02

A new strategy for new challenges

In exploring the topic of strategy, it becomes evident that, as leaders and practitioners, we are constantly searching for ways to organize and categorize our thoughts and thinking into something that closely resembles coherence. But why and for what purpose? It seems to me that strategy is often only considered at the most senior levels of an organization by the highest paid company employees, and then it is often only communicated and shared within a relatively small and exclusive group of executives.

During the development phase, strategy, as I've found in the research for this book, can very quickly turn into a mundane and unimportant exercise that has quite limited impact across the whole business. Usually, this happens because the business is not entirely engaged in its creation nor is it highly consciously involved in its delivery. It is 'owned' by a function or group of functions and can be developed in near total isolation based on what a few people feel is best, based on their own specialist expertise and their narrow view of the organization. This isn't the worst-case scenario by any stretch. There are many companies that do very little thinking about aligning actions, resources and behaviours to drive long-term results. In those situations, everything happens by chance or through organic, sometimes haphazard, development, and what will be will be. Now, I am far from against organic organizational development, but I am also heavily in favour of thoughtful, intentional and considered design, but can the two sit comfortably together? We'll explore this as we move though the book and the ideas being presented. But this may not be a typical strategy book in the traditional sense, because what I've uncovered and learnt is that employee experience (EX) strategy is not created in the typical way that strategy is developed, shaped and delivered. Indeed, an EX strategy is a different beast altogether, and rightly so if we want to truly connect strategy to the people that execute and experience it.

Unravelling people strategy

It's interesting how quickly things change. Many elements and parts of people strategies that were once cast in stone have been unravelled at lightning pace over recent years. Every major 'norm' across the employee experience has been under intense scrutiny and challenge by a pandemic that no one asked for, and consequently, no one had prepared for. There is very little, if any, precedent for what has occurred in organizations. Finally, the word transformation can be used in its truest sense. Transformed organizations have emerged that have ripped apart and reset how work gets done and how work is experienced by their people. It has, of course, been a time for experiments, for trials, for pilots. It has also been a time of friction, tension and unrest within companies given significant societal challenges, including a cost-of-living crisis with soaring gas and energy prices alongside increasing food prices, which have led to a period of high inflation. People are being squeezed from almost every angle, and to continue as business as usual given these compounding challenges is wishful thinking at best.

This is because the employee experience is locked hand in hand with the human experience. What happens over there will impact over here. They are robustly connected and to treat them in any other way completely misses the point and will lead to negative outcomes. That being said, there are also incredible opportunities for businesses to create experiences that inspire, engage and elevate people to new levels. But there has to be a strategy behind them. This is not haphazard and accidental work. It is defined, designed and delivered.

When strategy is done well, it considers the employee experience as a holistic idea rather than fragmented parts. Yet this is the most challenging aspect – to see the whole picture and to connect the dots across businesses chasing multiple targets, objectives and priorities. It's not easy to get things right, and it's not the easiest thing in the world to get people aligned and moving in the same direction. This is where strong strategy and weak strategy stand apart. The former can be confusing, incoherent and pointless. The latter can be the foundation stone that helps unite an organization around the things that matter most when it comes to business and human performance.

The dysfunctional employee experience

The EX Achilles heel and the subsequent downfall of any EX approach is a lack of alignment. Of all the issues, challenges (perceived or real) and missed opportunities that I've observed in companies, alignment remains the number one concern to be addressed in my view. Whatever comes after is a long way behind alignment. It's a strategic misstep in a category all of its own. It is worth singling out alignment for some closer inspection, especially as we start to navigate the strategic challenges that EX presents. It's so significant a risk (or opportunity) that I would encourage companies to frame up the entire EX strategy around achieving it as a significant win, victory and outcome. A good strategy will deliver that – aligned actions, decisions, and decisions that progress the EX and the business.

Far too often though, alignment is not chased or cherished with the level of intensity it deserves and warrants. The surprising thing from my perspective is that this is entirely understandable and I have some empathy with leaders and practitioners in this regard. If EX is viewed as a HR thing, seeking and achieving alignment beyond that specific function is hard. Even shaping and securing alignment within HR presents its own challenges given the diversity of roles, specialisms and agendas. For example, a learning and development (L&D) professional or HR business partner may not immediately see the connection between their work, the EX and brand outcomes. More broadly, an IT manager may not be aware of the impact that their work has on the EX and how it connects to the Truth – purpose, mission, and values – of the business (Whitter, 2022), and why that even matters. The other matter to be quite candid about here is time. It takes a lot of patience, skills and empathy to join the dots and create connections beyond immediate colleagues. It's a lot of effort to drive alignment through the business and requires management discipline.

We cannot simply continue with the status quo on this either as alignment doesn't always magically happen over time (it might do if you get lucky and things naturally connect up), so it needs to be engineered, to be orchestrated and to be targeted as part of the EX strategy. A new approach to building great experiences takes time, patience and a bag full of effort. Often, the work starts with a dysfunctional organization. That's not to say there isn't a foundational people strategy in place with the related specialisms. Quite the contrary; companies can be quite advanced in their HR approaches while, at the same time, quite immature in EX terms. I've noticed award-winning employers being heralded for some of their people projects, and rightly so, celebrate small wins along the way. Yet, looking into these companies in a more meaningful way leads to the discovery that all is not well under the surface.

The main issue is that employee-facing services are not aligned and being guided by a consistent set of principles, and perhaps an over-arching philosophy on how the business creates, moves and reacts over the course of its life cycle. There is not a time that this is not more obvious than at times of crisis. The mask slips and we see what companies are really all about. As an observer, I see the good and the bad. I still applaud specific aspects of the EX at companies that have been dragged through the public square because of other issues in the EX. I realize that no company is perfect, but I'm still inclined to push boundaries to ensure the EX is performing to a high level in all aspects. It's an interesting dimension of this work.

One company springs to mind on this; it was headline-making for the wrong reasons based on several leadership scandals and evidence that indicated somewhat of a toxic workplace. At the very same time, its Glassdoor rating – the platform where employees can rate, review and rank their employers – was a very healthy 4.4 out of 5. We can condemn specific actions, decisions and approaches, but to condemn an entire company and all of its people and EX is a bridge too far for me.

I recall a multinational corporation that was investing heavily into the EX. It was a full-on commitment and enthusiasm was very high from the leadership team and the people working to improve the EX. A very firm public commitment was given by the CEO about developing the EX. Things were progressing well, but unbeknownst to the EX team, a decision was in the works that would set that early work back considerably. The management team decided to abruptly withdraw the annual bonus scheme and they also failed to communicate and explain that decision to the workforce. The decision took the organization, and the EX team, by complete surprise. It hurt people badly, they felt let down, and all the promises being made about the EX were then subject to extreme cynicism. All that good early work undone with one decision. If the decision is in the interest of the long-term health of the business, employees can understand and accept that if it is communicated wisely, but to drive this experience through in this manner – and believe me, it was an emotional experience for those involved – is disrespectful and the complete opposite of what we are trying to achieve with EX.

This is why alignment between leaders and employees is such good work to do upfront and early within EX work. Decisions taken in isolation have the potential to rock organizations to their very foundations. It is also indicative of a fragmented and misaligned organization, as this sequence of events is quite common across management lines. Functional leaders touching the

EX are a team. In the early days of the EX strategy, they may not even know that each other exist, let alone connect their objectives. With EX, I look at all employee-facing functions and their impact on the EX. It is a shared agenda for the organization, but even now, after several years of implementation, this remains a serious pain point within EX work and is something we ought to explore more fully. I'm not talking about getting people in a room as and when required for EX projects. That is weak and won't suffice over the long term.

Small moments, big impact

The word strategy often conjures up thoughts associated with big things. Strategy is considered to be something well above operational and day-to-day work. Employee experience turns this thinking upside down. Strategy in EX builds up, not down. It starts from the root and grows. Moment after moment. Interaction after interaction. These are the elements that are in scope, so in terms of this book, strategy is not far removed from people. It is right next to them. We will discuss strategic themes, planning and how to build up a strong strategy; yet we must not forget that when all is said and done, EX strategy is about delivering moments of real impact with employees. Systems, platforms and products will be part of the equation, but the focus must remain on people throughout all of our discussion and dialogue. Of course, employees welcome clear direction about the future and their objectives, and how those things affect their roles and performance – this is foundational stuff, but they are more concerned about the moment and delivering outcomes in their work and life. Why is this? Well, reason number one is that we are human beings. All we ever have is right now – the present. Past and future can lead to overthinking of the most destructive nature. Indeed, as companies grow or transform, anxiety across the workforce can creep in quickly and a good EX strategy will be the counterbalance to that.

It was always going to be a challenge to emerge successfully from a pandemic the size and scale of COVID-19, but the scale of the additional challenges in the human experience will push people and businesses to breaking point. Predictions of a 'long and ugly recession' are becoming all the more frequent (Bove, 2022). And even just the possibility of major banks like Credit Suisse and Deutsche Bank collapsing as a prelude to a major financial crisis beyond the magnitude of 2008 (Chung, 2022) is an indicator of the unease being felt in the business world right now. CEOs are feeling it too: 91 per cent of US CEOs believe a recession is on the near horizon and a majority of them are actively getting ready to reduce headcount (KPMG, 2022). This uncertainty, no doubt, will hit organizations and the people within them, hard. In fact, it already has. Indeed, the aftershocks of the global pandemic are still with us and many workers continue to be operating in survival mode according to the American Psychological Association. A 2022 poll indicated that all of the big global issues at the time of writing – the war in Ukraine, rising inflation and the cost-of-living crisis – have created the perfect storm for growing uncertainty and anxiety amongst workers (American Psychological Association, 2022). This leads to high stress levels and several other key side-effects including personal and performance issues.

A world in financial crisis

Reports in the US suggest employers won't get anywhere near to keeping pace with inflation when it comes to salaries, with a predicted average salary budget increase of just 4.1 per cent versus an inflation level hitting 8.3 per cent. This is stark. The last hope for employees to secure money that helps them ride out the cost-of-living crisis goes well beyond tightening belts – people are hopping to new jobs to increase salaries, which has fuelled the great resignation in recent years (Ito, 2022). In a red-hot labour market, employers will be looking at their salary packages; yet it won't be the magic wand that people make it out to be. Building an EX strategy on money alone will simply not be enough to attract and retain high-quality talent.

The cost-of-living crisis is a touchstone moment for all kinds of businesses. If there is no upwards movement on salaries or the quality of the overall EX, then people with options are already accessing them. It's not so much driven by ambition but by survival, given that every area of an employee's financial life is in scope for some serious stress. From mortgage payments, energy costs, right through to groceries, fuel price hikes and a whole lot more increases on consumer goods, employees are squeezed and stressed from all directions. No amount of love for their jobs, colleagues and company will be enough to retain people if they are struggling to meet their financial obligations. It's a serious situation and we'll need to be mindful of this when shaping ideas about the EX strategy amidst these highly uncertain times.

Any fluffy stuff went out the window a long time ago. In my view, EX is, and has always been, the best for business when it is unleashed to deal with great pain. No fence sitting. No indecision. Just pure, decisive action that is wholly designed to meet the moment. When employees are going through difficult times, this is where organizations can differentiate themselves from the crowd. It's a remarkable opportunity to actually live all of those wonderful words in a company's value statement and create authentic and enduring bonds with and between people. An EX strategy that ignores these challenges will come unstuck eventually.

Pain becomes power

EX strategy can very well be formed in the fire of pain. Crisis moments act as the catalyst to scaffold new ideas about how business gets done. All of the less than helpful projects fade into the background. As companies we are faced to square off with the things that matter, the things of most pressing concern and the things that employees really need help with. This is the time they need the strongest ally they can get, and employers can fill that role like nothing or no one else can. It's an almighty and galvanizing moment – an interaction that can define the perception of a company for years to come. Are we with our employees or not? The EX strategy will need to deliver an unequivocal yes on this front.

This is why EX strategy will need to explore pain in a whole new way. In bygone eras, the pain being referenced by employers was almost exclusively focused on company hours. Employers fixated only on the things that they could directly control within the traditional time-based boundaries of business hours. It was certainly a good start to support people and demonstrate care within work hours; some companies have not yet evolved to that point, but there have been many missed opportunities to influence outcomes beyond that. To do this, companies are reconsidering typical boundaries in relation to the wider human experience. This naturally reforms EX strategies and expands the influence of the company in the lives of their employees.

For leaders and practitioners, this means, in a practical sense, that good strategy may start with considering the employee, but it will not end there. Indeed, scaling humanity across the organization is a never-ending endeavour and one that will lead to some profound questions about the role of the company.

A talent shortage

The balance of power has shifted to the talented worker. It may have been there all along, but it is now there en-masse given there is a critical shortage of talent across the economy, and it is driving employers to consider their EX strategies in a serious way. Indeed, record employment levels means there are more vacancies than actual workers. This is hitting businesses hard as they seek to grow and build their workforces.

In the UK, the number of unemployed people was lower than the amount of job vacancies in 2022 for the first time in recorded history. The Office for National Statistics paints an interesting picture right now; alongside more job vacancies than unemployed people, the number of job transitions, based on resignation, hit record highs too. What's behind this? Well, a PricewaterhouseCoopers survey of 2,000 UK workers found that pay was the biggest factor (72 per cent) driving resignations and job changes. On both sides of the employment relationship, there is evidence of a large number of transactional relationships right now, and should a downturn arrive, companies and new hires will likely face a very precarious existence.

Changed lives, changed workplaces

The large-scale global experience in remote working cannot be simply swept under the carpet as if it didn't happen. Despite the best efforts of some companies, hybrid and remote working have moved forward as a key part and aspect of organizational design. Employees have demanded it, and in many cases they have secured it through different configurations of their work weeks. The current trial of the four-day week in the UK by 70 companies is yet another indicator of the support and willingness of companies to do something different in order to engage with their people whilst pushing productivity higher.

Without doubt, there has been a call to action on flexibility. Real flexibility in and of the workplace. Employees have consistently articulated the need for hours that better connect to their life and other responsibilities, as well as the flexibility to do their work in a way that suits them. The workplace now is certainly no longer defined simply as a building, which is a positive given how much work and productivity takes place away from the actual physical symbol of the enterprise, which has often been represented by the office.

With this comes challenges. A chasm has opened up between managers and employees, with the former expressing the view that employees can't be trusted to work efficiently and effectively away from the company's physical estate, and the latter feeling that they can and do work better in this new mode. These sentiments have been somewhat validated by new research from Microsoft. A survey of over 20,000 global knowledge workers found that the majority of managers simply do not trust people who work remotely and are not at all confident in their ability to be productive (Microsoft, 2022).

Leading a more conscious workforce

A striking example of a challenge that manifests itself across the employee experience is the almost authoritarian way in which companies shepherd their employees into a pre-determined path of choices. A menu of items that employees can access or utilize is often forced upon them and presented to them as if this was something that would satisfy their appetite for more freedoms in work. The scale of the challenge here cannot be understated given the level of change in expectations across workforces. Yet, there is also an undercurrent that the focus of companies is perhaps not always on the right things and outcomes. Profit and growth are being driven at an urgent pace for overarching outcomes that are not clear, and in some cases are not necessarily positive for humanity or the world around us.

There is an illusion of choice taking place within firms in how they roll out their benefits, perks, and they tailor their employee experiences to suit the corporate rather than the individual's agenda. In other words, employees are given a set of binary choices that they really have no say in at all. This is not, in any way, personalization, but I do think some firms try to disguise it as such. The perceived advances in an employee experience, therefore, may actually be hurting a business because employees are not involved in the creation of their own choices. It is a rigged game and employees take action where and when they can as a result. The rise of employee activism at some of the world's top workplaces is a real-time indicator that sometimes an attractive EX can be delivered at the expense of something more positive and meaningful for employees.

Productivity is something that requires active participation; yet if experiences are not developed, aligned and incentivized, participation will be the obstacle to organizational success. People will simply check out rather than participate in a system that doesn't connect well to their thinking, and in the end, trends like the so-called 'quiet quitting' will become all the more frequent. Now, as an old friend at the top of the HR profession would say, this trendy focus on 'quiet quitting' is simply 'old wine in new bottles', and it really is. Engagement levels at a global level have been stagnant or in decline for decades. People would prefer to opt out of the system and not be part of it if their major needs are not being met within the employee experience. It's a constant negotiation between employee and employer. The pendulum will swing in favour of one or the other depending on the conditions of the labour market and the overall buoyancy of the economy.

Real personalization is when employees have the power to really choose how they experience their company and work. Beyond simply picking from a list of the company's preferred options, employees can, in every sense of the word, choose and come up with ideas on their own work life and run with them. We know that employees around the world have been activating new choices based on their own preferences and in much more alignment with their overall human experience, which would perhaps lend favour to the idea that employees are more conscious post-pandemic. They are more aware that life is not infinite and they are not indestructible – this then opens a pathway to explore the things and experiences that they really want, and the employer will either enable these new expectations or hinder them greatly.

From culture to lived experience and performance

The focus on organizational culture is still very much in its heyday, but it presents a big challenge. In *Employee Experience* (Whitter, 2022), I rarely mentioned culture and it has not featured heavily in my work to date. Culture is often inserted as a signpost to connect work and projects to something bigger. It is often spoken about for validation of EX work – the changes and improvements to EX drive the organizational culture, which in turn enables business performance. I think the time is right to take a more significant step back from this very woolly, vague and abstract idea that is often banded about in organizations to no effect. Employees don't talk about employee engagement, nor do they really spend much time talking about organizational culture – they care much more about practical and tangible things that become part of their lived experience. This is what matters most and this is where EX strategy should be focused. Along these lines, employees remain absolutely concerned about their performance and the performance of their company. It stands to reason that they are also sensitive to the performance of the EX.

Would it make more sense to position leaders and practitioners in alignment with performance and the lived experience rather than the much bigger and convoluted notion of organizational culture? This mirrors my work in the EX field. I can tell you very clearly that culture is rarely mentioned and when it is you can feel a sense of disconnection with the term – in practice, we are more targeted around EX performance and its connection to outcomes (for businesses and people). Culture is naturally created, enhanced and experienced by those who make a contribution to it through their decisions, actions and the things that they bring to fruition, so focusing on culture as the overarching big thing may not be as wise as it once was now that the more practical EX has emerged as a key management concept.

There is nothing more satisfying for an EX leader than transforming a moment of pain into a moment of performance. The bridge between these two outcomes is potential and organizational leaders are getting better at identifying and changing them. It's the litmus test of EX strategy – do things change in a positive way? Is the organization experienced positively by employees as they navigate their day-to-day experiences? Are they able to perform? It's a uniquely human thing to take something that is bad and turn it into something good, and this also happens to be a business-growing intervention. It means something to people if you take away their pain – not just say you will, but actually do it, or at the very least alleviate it in some way. Employers stepping in to offer additional support for employees during the cost-of-living crisis was a good example of this. A company was not in control of household energy bills and soaring costs, so they were not free to completely eliminate the pain being experienced, but some companies did meet the moment by providing financial support in the form of one-off or recurring bonus payments.

What happened here is telling; employers acknowledged the very real pain employees were suffering, and they tangibly stepped in to make a positive difference to that situation. Was that action just based on doing the right thing by employees? Was it strategically planned out? Or was it simply humane leadership at the top of organizations? In any case, it was a strategic decision to take action for employees and we'll need to think much more in terms of strategy flowing and unfolding in the lived experience rather than some abstract document that does nothing for anyone other than the executives that wrote it.

In that sense, strategy is forever evolving over time and through experiences. It is not a one-off cycle nor does it reach an end point. There may be timed elements in its delivery, but the process and practice of strategizing the EX continues indefinitely as long as there are employees and business outcomes to deliver. Certainly, when I think about strategy, I see, feel and experience movement. It is not stationary. It is not stagnant. It is a continuous process with outcomes being realized daily, for good or bad. The latter almost always being experienced when there is clearly a lack of strategic thinking and planning. Yet strategy requires people in a variety of roles to make a strong contribution, take ownership and lead in a collective, holistic manner, and not all leaders and professionals may be capable of that kind of thinking on a consistent everyday basis.

Life is the goal: do we really need purpose?

Reflecting on the experience of the last couple of years has led people to question the very foundation on which their existence is built. It's been a humbling process for many, and for some it has been truly shocking to discover what has been hiding in the depths of their mind. The notion perhaps of most exploration has been the idea of life. What is our purpose here? Do we really need to lead a purposeful life? Does any of that really matter? We are driven into so many default conditions, systems, rituals and behaviours that it's hard to keep track of what really matters. Getting the next promotion matters. Paying the next bill matters. Getting a good pension matters. Working hard matters. Living in a big house matters. Having lots of money matters.

Within all of this noise, I find favour with Kierkegaard's idea that 'life is not a problem to be solved, but a reality to be experienced' (Hipkiss, 1986). It is what it is, but in organizational terms, we can and must do better to create better lived experiences for our people. A sound EX strategy will seek to address and face the challenges I've highlighted here head-on, and if there is a purpose to life and indeed organizations, it is, in my view, to progress people and the planet. What we need to consider is the overall holistic in-context masterplan for EX that sets the organization up in the best possible way for EX outcomes. Having been through many iterations of this type of work for EX leadership teams, we can identify what needs to be present within such a blueprint from a strategic point of view, and we'll discuss that more in the next chapter.

03

Co-creating the employee experience strategy

Listening is only the start of the employee experience journey. If your strategy is only concerned with listening activities and exercises, then get ready for a very difficult challenge ahead. Every company has the capacity to listen, but not many have the capabilities required to really hear what people are saying, and then put in place the most impactful actions that address that. This is the far more important part of getting employee experience (EX) strategy right in practice. In theory, there are many techniques, tools and activities that can be used to listen to people, but the only thing that really matters is what is heard, acknowledged and acted on. Listening without action is as useful as an umbrella with holes in it. In the context of this book, the gaping great holes will appear in the EX strategy and it may well be too late to correct once the corporate machinery is invested in them.

I often listen to practitioners presenting their wares on employee experience. Setting out an EX approach quickly becomes detailed work with various techniques and technologies brought to the fore until eventually something sticks, something works in practice for the company's context. This can be distracting for practitioners and employees alike. The latest fads or age-old design or management thinking concepts are wheeled out in the hope of creating better experiences. Now, a lot of these can prove their worth, yet I feel the central message about EX can become lost in amongst all that. The technology, process or model becomes the major driver, not the people. The antidote to this, regardless of what's going on or the specialist tastes of those leading EX, is co-creation, and it is quickly becoming an organizational and leadership superpower.

Co-creation first: everything else flows from there

What is co-creation? Put simply, it is creating something together, rather than apart. For every leader, team and business unit, co-creation really must be the go-to start within their leadership playbook. Evidently, an unfaltering commitment to co-creation has emerged from the outset of the EX movement and it is only strengthening over time. Indeed, I have stated previously that co-creation is the foundation stone for any work on EX.

Is there really any more clarity that needs to be added on this topic? Well, there are clearly some disconnects occurring in practice when it comes to rolling out genuine, deep-rooted co-creation. The tendency for practitioners to work in isolation up until the point of consultation with employees remains a prevalent and undesirable practice. It also doesn't make a ton of sense when you think about the role of employees in using, accessing or experiencing the fruits of any well-intentioned EX project or programme. This could be a system, a product, an app or a service – all roads lead to the user (or to put it in a better way, experiencer) and their involvement needs to be consistently high throughout any programme of work. This is not always the case, for whatever reason. Busyness, urgency, fear, anxiety, lack of resource or internal pressure sometimes removes the employee from the co-creation loop – it's sometimes viewed as an unnecessary step to work with employees directly on projects, but I've seen first-hand that nothing could be further from the truth. Insights and direct involvement, in my experience both internal and external to organizations, has always enriched them. In fact, employee involvement has made EX projects the successes they eventually become. This is an inevitable consequence of working on real things that matter to people and also the business, not one or the other.

Another highlight of co-creation is that it feels good – it's an enjoyable part of the strategy development process to have your key stakeholders together helping you to solve their specific problems or challenges that are getting in the way of productivity and performance. For any support function, it is critical, but too often co-creation is light touch and insincere. It is a tick-box exercise rather than meaningful engagement, yet it is hugely advantageous to do this well and generates all manner of positive and secondary outcomes. Indeed, I challenge EX practitioners to deepen their co-creation activities as much as possible when and where they can within their portfolio of responsibilities. This chapter then serves as a reminder (and a warning) that co-creation is integral to EX and leaders would be wise to make this an enduring ingredient in their EX strategy efforts.

The co-creation partners within

There are a broad range of people and groups to co-create with across the organization, and having worked with colleagues across all these groups, I can tell you for sure that they all have pivotal parts to play in EX. 2022 was strike season around the world. I recall two experiences I had in London and Paris. At the former, I was booked to deliver a keynote address at one of Europe's leading HR conferences – it was apt that it took place in the middle of a national rail strike. I adapted my travel and found a way to honour my commitment, yet I couldn't miss the irony of speaking about EX on such a difficult day for workers and those who were affected by strike action. In Paris, I found the same and arrived to deliver an EX workshop on the day of a general strike. Such strong disagreements between workers and their organizations are not pleasant for anyone to experience. Activism has a rich history in the development of our economies and workplaces. and without people taking a stand about fairness and equality, employees would not enjoy the standards they do today. Yet activism represents a breakdown of the relationship between companies and their people, and should be avoided. If that is not possible, then it should be embraced and activists should be welcomed as co-creation partners too.

For EX leaders, the primary co-creation groups are (in no particular order) shown in Table 3.1.

TABLE 3.1 Co-creation groups

Co-creation group	Why?
Senior management/ Executive team	Align to the vision of senior executives and the future direction of the business.
Employees	Align with the needs and wants of the permanent workforce.
Customers	Align to the core needs and expectations of customers and consumers.
Workers	Align to the needs and wants of the growing workforce made up of contractual, contingent and gig workers.
Unions	Seek alignment on key developments that affect employees and the business/organization.
Functional heads	Align agendas to create products and services that enhance the EX and enable the EX strategy.
All leaders	Align and enable strong leadership and cultural performance through the EX strategy.
Employee/worker activists	Those disgruntled with an organization can be the source of much insight. They are a valid co-creation group, not an enemy.

What I've noticed, and which has been a constant in my work on EX, is the shift from stakeholder management to co-creation leadership. Stakeholders are there to be managed, co-creators are there to make a contribution. Too often in business, there is a detachment from work that affects employees, which leads to passive involvement at best. We've found a better way is to double-down on roles, responsibilities and accountabilities. There will be a time to listen to each of the key groups, but then they will need to make the transition to co-producer of the EX, and indeed, the organizational culture. There are levers, of course, to firm up such responsibilities in EX work like incentives and rewards, but in many companies, internal projects are the opportunity that allows the real organizational culture to shine right through.

Rejection is an important feature of this too. When taking proposals for approval, there can be knockbacks, concerns, or plans can even be completely derailed by the management team, or one (or several) influential director(s). An EX investment might come under some scrutiny, a programme or service could be challenged, or the design of an experience could come under some fire. How you, as an EX leader, see these things matters a lot. Getting rejected by anyone or anything can be deflating and lead to stress, anxiety and perhaps check-out behaviours, so we need to be ready for this. I can tell you now that the single biggest shift in my career took place when I saw these rejectors or cynics for what they truly were... co-creators.

Articulating what EX means to your organization

We'll start to look in more detail at all the components of a well-rounded EX strategy in the next chapter and mapping those elements out will be some productive foundational work as they will all feed into this section directly, which centres on making EX work for your company, context and culture. No doubt, there will be some good work on EX happening around the business, yet if every function and colleague is off on their own adventure, the EX strategy may fail to live up to its potential. This is potentially the trickier part of EX – bringing together a diverse range of people and backgrounds to contribute to an organization-wide agenda. This is also where we establish that a successful EX playbook from one organization may not do well in a new context and company. In that sense, mimicking is out of the question and we'll need to articulate EX for our unique conditions to arrive at a definite statement of:

- what EX means to your company
- who owns EX and who contributes to it
- where the accountability sits for key moments along the employee journey
- roles and principles underpinning all EX interventions and developments.

Without this level of understanding, it will always be a fragmented and disconnected experience despite the best efforts of all concerned.

The useful cynic

Sometimes plans can sail through the approval line and be a complete disaster because no one really cared enough to challenge them at management team level, and no one really backed them when they came into practice and were developed into the business. If plans are being rejected, someone is at least paying attention. That is good! That is also co-creation because you would hope senior leaders have arrived at the top team with sufficient wisdom and experience that will help you, as an EX leader, deliver a strategy that can actually get implemented successfully. For this, you will need many of the top team leaders and their people to get behind the EX work as a serious part, and enabler, of the overall business strategy.

To underline this some more, great EX strategy is not in any way about you, or any other EX leader. It is about the business and its people. Therefore, both parties will need to lead it, together. The reason people get placed into EX roles that evolve EX strategy is to help guide strategy, shape strategy, cultivate strategy, and in the end, to help install the strategy successfully into the business, but this is not a sole responsibility and nor should it be treated as such. Yet, as we'll come to learn about in later chapters, EX leaders have leaned into a far more effective skill and capability set in recent years that helps them to do their job to an exceptional level, and I dare say that their businesses would be in a much weaker position without their particular sets of skills and leadership style.

A high-quality start

The success of the EX strategy is largely determined by the quality of those first few months working on it. Sometimes, leaders are given time and space to really go deep in creating a long-term, enterprise-level strategy, so the duration of this stage will vary depending on the size, scale and scope of each company. I've worked with vice presidents (VPs) that have had anywhere from one month to upwards of 12 months to go through this stage of strategy development. The duration of this phase will come down to the context of the company, but the steps leaders go through rarely change. They get to work on their big EX challenge and they start to create their own LUCK in the process.

The great part of EX strategy work, in my view, is to craft something compelling that is directly tied to business strategy. It's a time to think about both bold and realistic moves, and to ready the organization for genuine employee-centric change. It requires a huge amount of LUCK, but not the type of luck you're thinking about. From our perspective and that of the practitioners I work with, we co-create our own luck by doing a few simple things really, really well at the outset of developing the EX strategy for a business. In this chapter, I will start to break these down in a way that can offer some insight on where you should focus first when working on EX strategy, and perhaps a few of the different ideas I've come across that sets EX practitioners apart from their peers.

To help frame the actions that leaders take when crafting their EX strategies, having a bit of LUCK on our side could be helpful. LUCK in this context means:

- Listen
- Understand
- Connect
- Kick-off.

Listen

By far one of the greatest strengths of EX leaders is their ability to listen at levels scarcely seen in the workplace before. I mean, these folks truly listen. In this part of the strategy development process, they are only concerned about listening to people. In their first few days and months in role, the amount of listening they get through is staggering, but who are they listening to and why does it matter?

In the organizational context, there are a quite a few groups that hold sway over business direction, business ethos and overall business culture. I've found it is wise to be balanced and listen across all of the different co-creation groups that I've mentioned rather than placing one over the other. Certainly, in our work, the employee is important, but that's only because the employee has, historically, not been as important to the overall business as they should be. So, too, are senior executives and the most senior employees. These people have emerged as the organizational leaders and should be afforded the respect they have earned by being role models for the company's purpose, mission and values. Given their impact on the overall direction of the company, they will be a key concern in the listening process.

Employee experience as a management concept has addressed the attention imbalance that existed previously; this idea that only customers matter has been found out. Employees matter more these days, but that doesn't mean we are employee-centric to the degree that we ignore or exclude any other groups. Indeed, any human who interacts with a business is important and there is much to learn from them, especially customers. An excellent development within the experience economy has been the strongly developing connection between work on the customer and employee experience – as fields, they have begun to converge and cross-fertilize each other to produce better business results. It's still early days, but many customer experience (CX) practitioners are thinking more about the EX space, and vice versa, which is welcome and will enrich outcomes.

Understand

In one global business I worked with, a VP of EX was appointed to lead an enterprise-wide approach to EX. They were a long-time leader at the company, operating consistently close or near to the top team of a multi-billion-pound market-leading company. It was only when they started this process of digging for, dissecting and analysing information that they realized there was already an EX team formed and in place, and the team had been operating for a good while, clearly well below the corporate radar. Fascinating, yet indicative of the complexity of large organizations. However, this was a high-performing leader who astutely and methodically worked through the organization chart to uncover any team, function or person that was working on EX. That understanding was critical in the early stages of EX, as a lot of good work was already happening that could be harnessed and brought to the fore to serve the wider business.

If there was a roughshod approach that disregarded this work, impact and progress, you can imagine what it would do to morale and the climate around teams, so there will always need to be a sensitivity and empathy for the work that has gone before us. That's not to say everything you find will be fantastic; some of it might be very poor and be delivering very little value, and tough decisions will need to be made to focus on other priorities that really matter to people. Leading with an employee-centric mindset will provide the business case for most changes in strategic themes, pillars and tactics, alongside the alignment to the overarching business strategy and direction, and all of this starts from a place of deep understanding.

Suffice to say, this is not a rush job that can be skipped. It's a serious part of a leader's first few months exploring EX within the context of their company, and will cover a myriad of things that are integral to the business, but what is produced during this stage is worth it.

Connect

Without doubt, one of the biggest challenges when it comes to EX strategy is alignment. Aligning people, decisions, investments and resources that bring about successful EX adoption is not easy by any stretch. Now, in the main, I'm an advocate of choice and personalization when it comes to EX. I frequently advise companies to invest as deeply as they can in this regard using a combination of technology and high-impact experiences to tune into the emotional frequency of their employees, especially at critical life moments. Companies may well be scratching their heads on this, as they invest in EX yet still they can be faced with regrettable attrition, or worse, people who stay and seek to bring a company down from the inside by giving nowhere near their best performance at work. They have good reason to hold back – there may be an issue that riles employees and the employer response that comes with it.

It's a complicated world and an even more complicated human experience, largely because we make it so. Simplicity is not usually held up as a status symbol for living life. So, how do companies ensure that their EX strategies are aligned to the things that matter? Well, in my experience, if employees are now starting to set their own boundaries in relation to their work life and their expectations alongside that, companies will need to modernize too, and fast.

For this, the organization and planet (OP) framework sets the tone for the modern company. Our EX strategies lean towards behaviours and contributions, and these will now need to be further targeted in companies, given the scale and nature of the challenges being faced by people and the economies and societies in which they work.

A non-negotiable within EX is that there is a serious effort by leaders to connect things up and present a united, well-branded and well-aligned strategy. Misaligned actions and intent create a chaotic and incongruent mess of things that is confusing to insiders and outsiders. No one knows what matters because strategies are disconnected and colleagues have weak bridges to one another. There is, in practice, very little joined-up thinking and movement takes place in all manner of different directions. There may be some hits amongst that, but the broader potential of EX as a business transformer never truly materializes because leaders are protecting what is theirs and building their own mini empires at the expense of wider company goals. This is where strategy execution falls down. It doesn't consider what connects colleagues and their interests, and, therefore, does not incentivize, reward or recognize behaviours that are good for the whole.

Connection – genuine connection – is always a positive aspect of team work and good human relations. Once connected, we can operate with candour, respect and strong collaboration – things get done in a better way, and the company benefits greatly by producing richer, deeper and longer-lasting outcomes. An IT team working effectively with an HR team on the digital experience is a good example here. The digital EX creates some natural cross-over points across these two services, so working hand in hand is a truly powerful step. This is in contrast to approaches I've experienced that keep these two domains separate. An IT implementation is never just a project to install new technology. It is a project to help people do and deliver better work.

Kick-off

In a lot of company scenarios, the kick-off for any project comes far too early. There tends to be a big kick-off event with invited parties and a lot of pre-thinking and formulating is shared, which in truth, does not have much use other than as a social event. Now, I thoroughly enjoy taking a piece of blank paper into a room filled with employees to canvas their views, reflections and ideas, but for me, this is part of the previous three stages. We listen to employees, we understand them, and we connect with where they are and where they would like to be. Only then can we start to think about doing a wider kick-off for the EX strategy around the organization.

It is very helpful for practitioners and leaders who are tasked with crafting the EX strategy to furnish themselves with the latest information and data on EX performance first, as they will need to get into the right headspace to help the organization (and its people) make sense of itself. I've covered how they do that in previous paragraphs, but it remains important to get this right to avoid some early pitfalls and gaps in strategy development. If we're wanting to develop EX strategy, it makes perfect sense to be employee-centric from the very start of the process, which means that employees take centre stage.

With any new work on EX, there is excitement and energy. It feels like great work to do and there is an urgency to assemble the right people to get things moving. For some inexplicable reason, employees are often left out of this early work. Yes, a team is gathered with the right mix of responsibilities to hammer out some form of connected and coherent strategy to develop the EX, yet there is often a lack of representation from employees at this critical juncture. It is powerful to have data and intelligence to inform strategy, but I would encourage leaders to take this a step further so that employees help to directly craft the overall EX strategy and approach. A key point is that EX strategy would be implemented more effectively if wasn't 'done to' the employees, but rather 'created with' employees. Just isolating this point highlights two distinct and starkly contrasting approaches. How can a company claim to be truly employee-centric if no employees were involved directly in crafting and shaping the strategy? EX strategy done well feels like a collective approach that is owned by employees rather than any one function or role.

In that sense, distributing leadership and securing wider commitment to EX objectives is simply a continuation of how we have approached EX so far. We just keep deepening and enriching the process of co-creation and this spills over into any programme or agenda that aims to kick-off EX as an organizational approach. It is to the detriment of the organization that strategy is formulated exclusively at the hands of a small collection of senior executives. It is not their strategy. It is everyone's strategy, and viewing strategy development in this way eliminates many future and preventable issues in the realm of strategy execution. People get it, because they made it. It is a defining point of EX organizations because it aligns business philosophy with tangible and visible actions. This is not a quite statement either. It is a loud signal of intent to the organization. It says employees matter so much to the business that any strategy that impacts them and their futures demands their attention, accountability and involvement.

This brings home a fundamental truth about employee experience. Employees will need to lead it from top to bottom, and be enthusiastic and energized by the work to move it to a higher level of quality. Indeed, when I have encountered weak employee experience approaches or projects, the related involvement level of employees has been low. This is unacceptable by any standard. It's like designing a car without the driver in mind throughout the process, or building a product and not thinking about the user in any depth and detail. Employees lead successful businesses through their contributions. Without them, very little good happens. For that reason, they must be an integral part of any EX work.

Transforming with empathy

Employee experience remains a never-ending journey of discovery and reinvention. It is this way because of the pace of change within society and the economy, and companies need to keep up with rapid movements in employee expectation management in much the same way they keep up with latest trends and insights related to the consumer experience.

Cynicism is a huge hurdle to overcome when transforming culture. So many decisions, actions and outcomes to get right throughout the employee experience and it starts with a firm and resolute commitment from the top. Without that, severe challenges await. With that, great things happen fast, for everyone.

As Kathleen Hogan (2022), Chief People Officer at Microsoft, points out, 'working alongside our CEO Satya Nadella to transform #Microsoft's culture has been one of the most rewarding aspects of my role as CHRO. Witnessing his commitment to making Microsoft a great place to work and the positive energy his empathetic leadership brings never ceases to inspire me.'

Having worked with executive teams at dozens of companies during the pandemic, I can tell you that the path to creating EX strategy in these circumstances is far from easy. We know that, don't we? It's not been easy for workers and employees through the pandemic, and it's certainly been a real challenge for all management levels. What we've seen has been nothing short of a major clash between styles, generations, expectations and the resultant top-down decision making. Some have forgotten the important principles of EX in the way that they advance strategy. This is problematic and has created mistrust and unrest across, under and between management lines. Too much standardization and there is no room to breathe. Too much personalization and decision making by managers and there are consistency issues. A good EX strategy will need to bear all of this in mind and satisfy all stakeholders.

Researching the EX is a holistic endeavour in that we are looking across the company for data, insights and information that will help us improve EX performance. Nothing is off limits if it adds value to our work on EX. It's the same with co-creation. The organization is a treasure trove of willing co-creators at all levels of the business. Even the not-so-willing will be helpful in this journey, but we'll need to adjust or adapt our mindset if we are to make the most of this.

Hopefully, your strategy development work will fail, and fail again, and keep on failing until there is an EX strategy that the business can collectively work with. However, the first response to perceived rejection or failure is not a positive one, for good reason. A lot of work may have been done to get a coherent strategy presentation or report to the management team, and perhaps it is rejected, or rejected with notes/feedback. Is this a good or a bad thing? I would rather not waste my time driving something through approval and funding processes that had little buy-in from senior leaders. This is not an effective or impactful use of time. The talk of a bottom-up approach is noble, yet reality is something different. We need our top leaders to lead EX.

There are a wide range of options when it comes to co-creation. I view *any* action as a contribution to developing the business, and by default, co-creation. The only thing that changes is the role, extent and depth of the contribution to the overall EX work. This can be a managed or informal contribution so the list below reflects my much wider approach to co-creation. I'm not simply talking about formal design and prototype workshops, which usually only involve a small number of employees or functional specialists. This could be summarized as *where the real action is.*

- Employee (and customer) surveys (pulses, sentiment analysis, formal feedback mechanisms)
- Forums
- Employee resources groups
- Committee and management team meetings
- Town halls/All-hands meetings
- Workshops/design processes
- Special project teams
- EX functional leadership team
- Gemba walks (as discussed in Whitter, 2021)
- Drop-in sessions

- Ambassador teams
- Leadership 1:1s
- Technology interventions, including network analysis
- Gamified or incentivized activities
- Customer forums/workshops

A co-creation campaign

Done well, co-creation becomes the natural pathway to bringing new products, services and experiences into being. It becomes an encompassing approach to utilizing the strengths, skills and talent that exists within and beyond the context of the organization. It shortens any change curve and ensures any changes flow into the organization rather than being forced through it.

It does become a campaign too, based on the range and breadth of options and activities that can bolster the EX strategy and its eventual impact. It's the other side-effects that also add real value – the ability to demonstrate and role-model the kind of organizational leadership employees respond positively to – high empathy, high transparency and high trust-based actions and communication approaches. Indeed, at this stage of EX strategy we can reset relationships and refresh the organizational leadership approach. It's not a campaign to win hearts and minds, but it could be the catalyst to doing just that.

SUMMARY

I have rarely found resistance to solid co-creation campaigns. The challenge with co-creation is that it is underrated within the corporate world, or viewed to be too much hard work. Much easier to develop in functional isolation, consult and launch. That kind of approach belongs in another era and it is the one that will include the more traditional practices around change management.

Co-creation at its finest will replace the need for anything that even closely resembles change management, which I've found to be far too organization-centred and that stifles a lot of the great potential outcomes that can come from creating spaces for people to make their contribution and utilize their creativity. People are not brought into EX projects to be managed. They will be operating under principles that enable them to express themselves and take their ideas through to implementation. Employees see an organization that reflects their contribution and an experience that is made by their design.

Co-creation sets projects and companies apart. It is one of the purest points of differentiation that I can identify across the organizational landscape. If you want EX work to be good, involve employees. If you want EX work to be exceptional, ensure employees are co-creating it.

04

An ecosystem for employee experience success

An inevitable question that has arisen about employee experience (EX) is whether or not there is a playbook or blueprint that can be applied and replicated across different organizations. Is there a standardized approach that can be picked up by leaders and practitioners in their context that leads to strong outcomes for EX? Put simply, I live in a world where this is simply not possible and nor would we want it to be. Despite the efforts of others to conveniently package EX as a solution, a platform, a product or a playbook, it simply isn't desirable to do that. A one-size-fits-all approach to EX is as weak an approach as I can imagine to organizational design, development and leadership. Indeed, the best examples of EX that I've come across are distinctly different, unique and immersed in their own context. It would be a challenge of the highest order to even try to mimic or copy the approach, and why would companies want to simply copy another organization in the first place? The obvious answer is time and outcomes. Building on the work and success of others is a temptation few can resist when it comes to accelerating their growth and success curve, but there are pitfalls in this approach. A shallow and superficial EX can mask deep fragmentation, unrest and broken relationships, and it's not healthy for anyone to have the occasional positivity boost delivered by a one-off copied experience, rather than the long-lasting and sustainable outcomes that a holistic EX approach can produce if it is a genuine approach that seeks to strengthen trust, respect and relationships at all levels.

An ecosystem to enable evolution

I've found that a much more beneficial way to approach and apply EX holistically is to think about an EX masterplan and supporting ecosystem. This helps to set the tone for the work and lifts thinking to the appropriate organization-wide level. Thinking about the whole ecosystem around EX will naturally drive powerful discussion and dialogue, draw the right people to the EX strategy work, and be immensely helpful in enabling a high-performing EX when the time comes to deliver the strategy in practice. The challenge for many practitioners is that they have developed a narrow, specialist worldview. Whatever function or subject matter people have been schooled and conditioned in will come to the fore within the work on EX, and we need to harness that, but at the same time, guard against it. It may divert the EX into a weaker and more narrow proposition within the business, which would be in direct contradiction to what EX, in my view, is meant to be – a collective and shared endeavour.

As a holistic idea, EX benefits greatly from many contributors and co-creation partners – all of whom have different ideas, personalities and ways in which they approach their work. Rather than curtail or stifle those, the area I like to focus much more on is alignment, and it features heavily in any work I've done to stand up EX teams, projects or enterprise-level EX approaches. While I am steadfast in my belief that an EX playbook doesn't exist (and nor should it), I am equally robust in my view that a masterplan can be established successfully within the context of an organization. That is to say, EX as an approach or process can be brought to order in the form of an overarching blueprint for success on the inside of the business, and this connects strongly to EX strategy development, of course. This is in stark contrast to a general or standardized approach that acts as a one-size-fits-all model for EX. That won't do at all.

A universal approach to employee experience

As I set it out here, each blueprint will be original and based on the context, characteristics and challenges of each individual company. Some of the fundamentals that I explore with businesses revolve around creating a compelling purpose for EX, establishing deeply installed principles into the EX team and approach, and the co-creation of an organizational blueprint for EX, which develops the former alongside other aspects that enable colleagues to join the dots effectively and enhance their contributions across all employee-facing functions and touchpoints.

There is an undoubted focus and intensity in EX work. Leaders tasked with coming up with a solid EX strategy are put into that role because they know how to navigate the organization chart, they have the ability to connect and join things up, and they are able to influence outcomes beyond that of their role and usually the small team behind them. I've used the term experience architect to describe these colleagues and that tends to sum them up quite well to this day. Part of the role in shaping EX strategy is to help companies determine what needs to be built in the first place and to draw out the unique strengths of the company to ensure high differentiation in the talent marketplace. What is striking about EX strategy, and what separates it from others, is the all-out laser-like focus on the experience of work. Yes, the clue is in the title – we have fixed our sights on employees, their experiences and the strategy that enables them – but once something is turned over to the corporate world, there is an element of dilution and there are forces that would rather corporatize strategy and organize all the human feeling out of it. EX strategy, as I've found, is different in this regard. It leans into the core topic at hand and seeks to humanize all the parts of the business that it can reach.

In strategy terms, leaders working on strategy are not simply allocating resources and creating plans of action. They go much deeper and are more active in understanding the real nature of their companies. I haven't, in all my years working in the HR field, observed such devotion and dedication to bridging the gap between employers and their employees through a well-balanced human-centred business strategy. It is a commitment that goes unheralded, yet it is an ever-present factor in crafting a strong EX strategy.

Defining questions to consider

A few key markers that have emerged in EX strategy development over the years can be summarized by the following questions:

- How long does it take for strategy to transform into tangible and effective actions?
- To what extent have employees been involved in strategy development?
- How far does strategy go beyond the borders of support functions?
- How active and engaged are company leaders in overall EX strategy execution?
- How deeply is EX strategy installed and connected to the overarching business strategy?
- How many data points have informed the EX strategy?

Growing through strategic challenges

A point to note and underline about strategy development is that there has to be evolution built into it. This feeling like we're on a journey and that things will never be complete in the way that we expect them to has to become part of our approach. Perfection doesn't exist. We can get close to it; yet as soon as we do, time has moved on, and so have the expectations of workers, and even perhaps senior management. The strategic thought behind this is always on change and challenge. From these challenges, people have the opportunity to grow their capabilities and their imagination on how complex problems can be solved. Thinking in this way also enables leaders to experience life and the organization as it really is – imperfect and always in need of improvement.

The life is sometimes strangled out of an organization because it encourages everything to be correct, to be orderly and to be tidy. The reality of the life experience is far removed from this, and if you peek through the corporate veneer you will always find an imperfect human underbelly. This is as it should be and is an important part of strategy development. There has to be a serious space to play, to experiment, to challenge assumptions, and, most importantly, to get things wrong. EX strategy development literally resets the rules around failure. We have to fail and fail again to find the right ways to connect with the workforce. This is often permitted failure – it is designed into the strategy development process to prototype and test new ideas in real scenarios through pilots and trials.

Conversations that matter

Once companies have started down the EX path, it becomes apparent that tackling EX in a more holistic way is raison d'être of EX leaders. There is much learning to be done prior to reaching this point though, and various frustrations in executing EX strategy. This is why I immediately put forward the holistic employee experience (HEX) model in earlier works because it was paramount to EX success. It would have been easier and more expedient to suggest EX was a simple design process, communication approach or branding exercise, but it isn't, so I double down here again when thinking about creating solid EX strategies. The need to consider the organization holistically only grows as the years go by, and things become more complicated especially if companies are growing at pace or transforming their business operations. Thinking and leading in a holistic and intentional way is a foundation stone of great EX leadership – the focus on the whole rather than the parts – and it will continue to be the case as organizations roll out and mature their EX approaches.

Timely examples of this emerge all the time. Businesses tend to hype their growth journeys and not think about the consequences until they need to. They are left brutally exposed during a downturn in the economy and then the real pain is experienced, most notably by employees with massive job cuts and scaling back of operations. In the past year, many industries have been affected by layoffs and there continue to be question marks about the way companies grow at such a furious yet unsustainable pace. Many of the major tech companies have announced major work-force reductions in recent times, and many have been found wanting in their ability to manage transitions and exits, or as I think of them, evolved relationships.

Deepening the holistic approach to employee experience

What tends to happen in practice is that there is a surge in enthusiasm for EX and projects are stood up to affect and enhance the experience of work for people. Some hits and some misses follow, and then a re-grouping takes place around a clear need to align people more closely on the outcomes of EX work. EX consists of many diverse ingredients, yet when too many chefs go after their own ideas and fail to connect the dots and unify actions and outcomes across the employee journey, then EX performance will be severely impacted.

This is perhaps the main reason that I up front the discussion and dialogue about the HEX and seek to get started on these inevitable issues before they bring progress to a grinding halt later down the track. A sincere and honest assessment will need to take place early on about the problems being experienced within the organization. Some can be fixed; others will take time and a serious trust-building effort within support services and much deeper into the company's approach to EX. This is generally where the marketing spin fades and you get a proper sense of what the organization is really all about. Reality for some organizations will be hard to navigate, especially if there has been a bias to branding and marketing at the expense of much more substantial organizational development and design work.

Inevitably, to develop an EX strategy, we'll need to start with the most basic of strategic questions about the EX at an organization. For me, I always return to the HEX for guidance and challenge. This is the strategic map and tool of choice to facilitate improvements, strengthen connections and eliminate weak spots. It's the model and tool I use most frequently around a business when talking to business leaders. They can quickly grasp, discuss and diagnose issues within it, and also key areas of strength. As a co-creation tool, it prompts insight, introspection and innovation because it brings people up from the surface of their work to consider the whole and how each element interacts with each other to unify and develop positive experiences. Deeper than that though is its ability to prompt reflection about the extent to which each element of the HEX is supporting the organization to achieve its mission and its people to achieve their goals.

For professionals working on EX, this is extremely important at the outset of their projects. This, as I've found in my work, sets up a point of difference between EX professionals. Some consider the whole when working on their projects, and some don't. The best results I've seen are unanimously associated with those EX professionals that connect their work to the greater whole – they manage to take their projects, plans and priorities deep into the organization and reach colleagues that others don't. This isn't as much a skill as it is a daily practice – a daily habit. But what are they considering at the very start of their projects? What are the key questions they run through in order to secure the best outcomes for whatever activity they are working on? And by activity, I use this term broadly to emphasize the diverse range of tasks that professionals work on that interact with employees – it is widely encompassing and is tied to anything and any professional that affects the EX through their work. A new or improved policy, plan, platform, product, tool, system or a wholesale experience redesign. Indeed, any initiative or intervention that touches the EX is in scope, and these questions rise to the surface quickly to help colleagues create the impact they set out to.

When starting a project that affects the EX, use this checklist of questions to refine your approach and build unrivalled consistency across your teams and companies.

TABLE 4.1 HEX strategic questions

HEX element	Strategic questions
Human	• Are you being as human-centred as possible in the design and roll-out of this project? Is the human experience (as well as the employee experience) at the forefront of your mind? • Is co-creation a fundamental and defined principle within your approach? Is this project co-produced with employees? • Are you designing and developing this project holistically and seeking to enrich it through collaboration and by connecting to other functions/colleagues beyond your immediate team?
Leadership	• Are you enabling leaders, as a collective, to drive this EX project into their daily (or habitual) management interventions and leadership practices? • Is the leadership team (at all levels) held to account for the quality and performance of this project and their team experience (TEX)? • Are leaders aligned to, sponsoring and championing the project?
Community	• Is belonging, and the creation thereof, a core and intended outcome of the project? • Does this project create a connection between their people and the communities around them? • Are there communities embedded into this project? Are they immersed, informed and inspired by the potential project outcomes? • Is there a clear and compelling communication plan behind or connected to the project to amplify impact and inclusion?
Structure	• Are all targeted and affected employee-facing functions aligned, organized and accountable for outcomes related to the project? • Are there sufficient roles and responsibilities to effectively lead and scale this project across the organization? • Is the employee voice effectively structured in to this project? Is your project structure agile and informed by real-time employee feedback, data and intelligence?
Technology	• Are the right products and services in operation to deliver a seamless, effortless and joined-up effort to support your project? • Is there sufficient intelligence, enabled by technology, to monitor EX performance of your project in real time? • Is your project driven by humans, rather than technology, and is the ecosystem in place to produce and sustain desired outcomes?

(continued)

TABLE 4.1 (Continued)

HEX element	Strategic questions
Workplace	• Have you considered the optimum configuration for employees' work and life in relation to your project? • Is the project aligned to flexibility and supportive of different work styles and personas? • Are you making the most of the spaces and places that your organization defines as the workplace? Are employees truly connected to your project in a way that enhances their experience of work?
TRUTH	• Have you connected your project to the brand's purpose, mission and values? • Have you ensured that your project continues to immerse employees into the values of your organization? Does this policy exemplify what your company stands for? • Does this project offer evidence that your company is living its Truth?

Employee experience strategy: a marathon delivered in sprints

In the world of employee experience and other fields dealing with design, strategy is nothing but a series of sprints that create strong and almost immediate outcomes. Redesigning or transforming a service, changing something about the employee journey, creating powerful moments of interaction at well-timed intervals and milestones in the life of an employee – these are the sprints that inject speed, sharpness, urgency and quality into the employee experience. Anyone who works in EX knows there is a strong bias for action within the field and across companies – people in or around EX leaning roles are motivated by getting things done and affecting early, significant and lasting positive change. Sitting behind these sprints is a strategic marathon – a long-haul thematic view based on a desired direction for the business and the people priorities that will help take it there.

Outcomes over opinions?

In EX terms, opinions forged through experience are outcomes. Generally, this plays out in reality like this: employees don't care about what you say you're going to do (though they will be disappointed with broken promises), but they do care much more about what they experience as a result of your leadership actions. For any EX strategy, it will make sense to start with the end in mind.

- What do you want people to feel as a result of your EX strategy?

Then again, opinions that are not our own do matter in EX as we have to take the evidence coming directly from key stakeholders very seriously. Two opinions are perhaps great indicators of how the EX is doing for real. These are the opinions from employees and competitors:

- In 20 years, what do you want former employees to be saying about your company?
- What would you like your competitors to be saying about your company and its EX?

A telecommunications company went on a two-year transformation programme that featured a radical revamp of the customer experience (CX) and EX, which resulted in record-breaking engagement and business performance levels, and re-established a legacy business once again at the top of the market. While feedback was notable from all quarters, of most note was the feedback I heard from its major competitor who said that what they did would have been perceived as impossible just two short years earlier. Impossible became possible, and the competitor also started to explore EX as a serious management approach.

It comes down to several things. Some will not be new to you as a way of developing strategy. However, there are some nuances in the way that we develop these areas from an EX perspective. Adopting agile is not a strategy. Adopting design thinking is not a strategy. Adopting a technology is not a strategy. These are merely things that enable the strategy. Nothing more, nothing less.

So, what is the strategy?

For me, the central strategy is the broad and overarching force that best enables the business to deliver its objectives. The connection points within this are based on a business leading in a holistic, human-centred and experience-driven way. Clearly, the strategic pillars that sit under this will change and be entirely dependent on the organization. In my experience, there are a wide range of themes that come through into the EX strategy, including simplification, empowerment, diversity and inclusion, belonging and well-being. What a company stands up as the strategic pillars is down to them and the priorities that their people have indicated.

However, in saying this, does it really matter? Do employees care about your strategic pillars and the themes within your PowerPoint presentations? The simple answer is no. They don't care about these things; they care about the results and actions that flow from these things. That's a big difference and one that many practitioners fail to comprehend. It's puzzling really that so much time and effort is spent on something that our target audience cares so little about. Indeed, this book would be futile if given to the average employee. They would have zero interest and that is fantastic.

Why? Because we don't want them to be distracted with EX strategy, with words, with rhetoric. We want them to experience and take part in driving the outcomes of EX strategy directly as co-producers. That's what a good strategy will do, but let's be honest about that. Half the time strategy is there to hold up or justify spend, and to monitor and report on progress. It's more for managers and senior leaders to crystallize their thinking and the commitments they make to each other and their people, and that's ok. I'm not one to promote or over-hype EX strategy – it plays a valuable role for practitioners and leaders, but it is not top of mind to employees.

Where does EX strategy sit and who owns it?

In launching or starting work on EX strategy, we have to consider this basic question: Who cares about employee experience? I would like to say EX strategy flows from the business strategy, and in theory it should. In practice, EX strategy can be condensed as a constituent part of the people or HR strategy, or at worst it can be a stand-alone strategy in its own right, which is disconnected from the core work of the business – a situation to be avoided at all costs. I'm not a fan of any separation between the business and what it does regarding employee experience. I see EX as the central enabling pillar of the business strategy. For some, this makes complete sense and is nothing new to note. For others, I suspect this would come across as wishful thinking if they were to consider their context, culture and top team. In saying that, a solid people strategy makes a big difference in practice, yet at times the focus on actual lived experiences is not where it should be – it can be drowned out by the noise of all the major priorities for HR. If like me, you lead the EX as a holistic construct, it becomes quickly evident where the weak spots are.

EX strategy is owned by the business so it should, ideally, belong as a core part of the business strategy. I can see the allure of the argument that if your top team ran the business in a holistic, human-centred and experience-driven way, there would be little point of a formal EX strategy. It would be strategy by default as long as it flows through management lines. This ideal-istic picture can hold true for small businesses, but with larger workforces it can often unravel quickly. A strong EX strategy then can play a solid part of business development, and this will leave us with some concentrated areas to rediscover and shape as part of our early thinking. For EX, I have spoken about the need for a MOVEMENT within the organization (mandate, oper-ating model, vision, energy, mindset, evidence, network and team) to firmly plant the seed of EX and maintain positive momentum. As I have supported companies to build their EX strategies and approaches, there are other prac-tical things we can also consider to complement this. Indeed, the backbone of any EX strategy will be the very things that underpin and help enable great work in practice from the team tasked with co-creating strategy.

'We're a big organization, we can't co-create everything.' Yes, you can, and you must, if you are to be successful with EX. I've already set my stall out for co-creation in the previous chapter. It really begins to surface as the primary approach the moment EX is spoken about seriously by senior management and there are early signals of intent through the appointment or repositioning of a senior strategic leader to get things moving and off the ground with EX. Invariably, there'll be a busy few months getting to know the organization and all of the experiences it delivers (or doesn't). I find the early introduction to EX follows a similar pattern of identifying and inter-rogating insights from inside and outside of the business. The temptation to learn from others further along in their EX journey is very strong, and company visits are often part of this discovery phase. Comparing and contrasting approaches is also helpful to nudge management teams in the direction of strong investment in the EX so there is a purpose for all this exploration within strategy development. Yet taking things too far and simply copying the EX approach of others or trying to replicate it at your company is not wise and is often a fool's errand. The best experiences are formed from deep within the context of the organization, not by mimicking the work of others.

Rather than give you all the answers here, I strongly recommend that you co-create them with your EX team to arrive at a contextualized blueprint for EX at your company. I see this blueprint as a living and evolving entity rather than a document dump for emails. We'll discuss how to enable it later, but that is the first principle: it evolves with us. The good news then is that it doesn't need to be perfect from the start, and actually I would only encourage use of headlines when working on this with the strategic EX team so that genuine co-creation can take place and wholehearted ownership can flow from there.

What does EX mean to you (and those leading EX-impacting functions)?

A clear first step when bringing together functional heads or strategic leaders with portfolios that touch the EX is to enjoy some debate about what EX actually means to your business. This step is often missed to the detriment of the organization. We want to avoid an articulation of EX that is forced upon strategic leaders – they have done no work on it nor have they contributed to it in any meaningful way. This is a strategic misstep of the highest order. If I want people to drive and lead outcomes on EX, they have to be aligned and accountable from the beginning of its implementation. But more than that. They have to feel that this is their approach, their work and their opportunity to make an impact that sits well in the context of their careers and work. It is not a side of the desk thing or an add-on to their real work. Having leaders go through the process of articulating what EX means to them and then converging around a common understanding is very often cathartic and sorely needed. Often, leaders with portfolios hovering around the EX have barely got to know each other, let alone work effectively together. Space, time and a little patience is required to work through this at the outset of the strategic work, and it sets the tone for what is to follow.

The perils of missing this important step – giving people space and time to reflect on EX – are massively underestimated. Without a shared experience of this nature, the strategic leadership group will remain a group and never have the chance to form as a team. This leads to confusion, lack of alignment, low commitment, frustration, and at best, an incoherent, disconnected EX. We do not want to make EX any harder than it is. For that reason, I favour dialogue and discussion as a way to build relationships and respect between management lines and across functional boundaries. There is a place for sticky notes and PowerPoints, but this isn't it. In fact, I tend to use reflective methods more than anything else when working on EX. A lot of the answers are already *in situ* – the problem is that no meaningful reflection takes place and insights are lost.

It's the same with data. Organizations ooze data. They are natural data machines. It is relatively easy to get lost in data within companies, but it's what comes from data that is of most concern to me: insight and action. So, reflection is a key tool within our locker to bring the insights out to play in crafting, co-creating and shaping EX strategy, and for that reason we need to schedule in time simply to reflect on the EX, the brand and the people.

Co-creation has already begun – building the blueprint for experience success

For strategic EX leaders, this is the more detailed part of strategy and team development, and I leverage my 8XP framework to articulate the priority parts that will require immediate attention at the outset of building the EX operationally. These are the specific foundational stones for EX teams. With the HEX hovering above at the strategic level, guiding our hand to deliver value and impact in the right places, 8XP is the strategic blueprint that supports the implementation of an effective EX strategy, team and approach – one that is enabled strongly into practice. 8XP consists of:

- people
- purpose
- principles
- pain experiences
- peak experiences
- processes
- platforms
- performance.

People: Creating and maintaining a universal approach to EX is a multidisciplinary, cross-functional effort. It's truly about people, not a person. Bringing functional heads and practitioners that interact with employees is critical in the early stages of the strategic work, and perhaps the most impactful work one can do to elevate the EX across an organization. In my facilitated workshops for executives, there is a diverse bunch of colleagues in the room or online – including functional heads from functions like estates, IT/digital, HR/people, marketing, benefits, branding, communications and customer experience. Clearly, these roles (and their teams) play huge roles at different (or all) points of the employee journey, and it is a prerequisite that they are involved in the EX strategy in some form. I recommend starting with the core roles that have the most impact on EX and we move from there as we'll also need to be hyper interested in those working on other core elements of EX like leadership, people and executive development, and any roles that influence the EX in a strong way.

Purpose: A unifying purpose for the EX and the EX team is necessary to bridge the gap between the EX and the organization. Both will need to reflect each other in practice. A strong purpose statement sets the tone for colleagues working on EX within an organization. We're really answering the question: What is the point of this work? What does my work have to do with EX and the business? So many colleagues across support services can inexplicably be left to their own devices to foster some kind of detachment from the organizations they serve. This has to stop and work on EX will change that entirely.

Principles: The primary outcome that I'm interested in when it comes to principles is what they enable people to do *in the present moment*. Indeed, the present moment is all we have, but our conditioning, education, experiences, background and training all influence and are brought to bear in the present moment. Principles are the guides that allow us to express ourselves and provide the foundation for actions, behaviours and decisions. In terms of EX, we want people to create decisions, designs, policies and practices that make a positive contribution to the EX, to people and to the business. I'm often asked in facilitated strategy sessions what a good principle for EX is. My answer is relatively straightforward in that any principle people can stand behind and actually implement *in the present moment* is a good principle. This widens the scope somewhat for the kind of principles that a team can adhere to and use to guide their work and impact towards the right places. I've highlighted a core set of fundamental principles for EX in my previous publications, and these remain highly relevant in terms of applying EX, but the right set of specific principles will need to be co-created into the context of the company. They can't be parachuted in from an external source in a clumsy copycat fashion. While reinventing the wheel is not always necessary, there are certain foundational things that simply do not warrant compromise, the non-negotiables, and developing some core principles for the EX team falls into that category, in my view.

That's not to say there won't be overlap with what other companies are doing – great companies tend to land in similar places when it comes to value statements, underlying and overt principles, and organizational missions. A strong set of principles is determined by how consistently they are implemented, modelled and utilized to lead. Amazon have won admirers in this regard. The company's now legendary leadership principles have been well integrated within and across the employee experience for leaders. The headline principles below demonstrate the critical areas that Amazon want to focus on within (and beyond) the leadership community, and they have been modified recently to accommodate new objectives relating to EX performance (see #15). Each of these is a description to guide people and their actions, and there is also a wide range of ways that these principles are communicated and enabled to create a more immersive (and real) experience around them.

1 Customer obsession

2 Ownership

3 Invent and simplify

4 (Leaders) are right, a lot

5 Learn and be curious

6 Hire and develop the best

7 Insist on the highest standards

8 Think big

9 Bias for action

10 Frugality

11 Earn trust

12 Dive deep

13 Have backbone; disagree and commit

14 Deliver results

15 Strive to be Earth's best employer

16 Success and scale bring broad responsibility (Amazon, 2023)

There is a tendency at times to overcomplicate principles; as we can see from Amazon, it's relatively simple language and is easy to understand. The application will evolve over time, but will show up in decisions and moments that leaders meet in their daily experiences, and the important aspect of this is that their progress will be measured against them and will count at the key milestones across their employee journey (promotions, recognition, etc.).

For the experience masterplan, I would be seeking to leverage existing principles that form part of the brand/business strategy or those associated with the people strategy (if and only if they are connected to the broader business strategy and employee value proposition, or EVP). This is what Amazon does well; they help leaders cross the bridge to the most important things that matter to the business, and customer obsession placed at number one is a strong indicator of that connection.

Pain experiences: Not all moments are created equal. For the EX masterplan to function properly, it needs to be disciplined around solving real problems and issues that affect the performance of people. The question is both political (I am reluctant to use that word, but that's what it is) and practical. The leadership within an organization will be grouping together to make decisions that change or challenge people's lives in and beyond work. So unifying around some core strategic themes that are viewed as urgent goes a long way to creating and sustaining a positive relationship with workers and aligning the EX team or collective towards some really tangible actions that will definitely make a positive impact. The trust outcomes here are immense. In all my work, there is nothing more powerful than taking away someone's pain. These experiences then have immense value in establishing and getting some real momentum behind EX. If you need some examples of painful experiences in work, search your memory banks, as I'm sure that there will be things organizations have done to you in your career that may have caused you some pain and resentment. If not, well, you're very lucky indeed, but ask three people and I would be surprised if you didn't have multiple anecdotes that pinpoint the kind of examples we're talking about here.

Peak experiences: The EX world has matured away from just fixing things that could work better though. World-class EX work increasingly revolves around the creation of peak experiences. A well-established phenomenon in the human experience where people truly come to life, feel joy and experience a profound moment in their lives. Many of these moments can be found at work and organizations have been lining up their EX teams to create signature, awe-inspiring, brand-differentiating moments at specific points along the employee journey. We're not encouraging forced joy here, far from it. What I am advocating is for organizations to set themselves apart in their sectors and markets by creating opportunities or windows that lead to much deeper emotionally connected experiences for their people. These moments literally rock people's worlds and almost guarantee brand ambassadorship for life.

Defining a peak experience

I defer to the solid work of Privette on this matter, who explored the unique characteristics of peak experiences after surveying a range of people about their strongest experiences in life. The result of this was the following explanation of what we mean by peak experiences.

- **Fulfilment:** Positive emotions are generated and are intrinsically rewarding.
- **Significance:** Personal awareness and understanding increase and can serve as a turning point in a person's life.
- **Spiritual:** People feel at one with the world and often experience a sense of losing track of time.

In my world of EX, data is not everything. Design is not everything. Decisions are not everything. They all impact, of course, but simply putting EX into one of these camps has never made any sense to me. Great design will not overpower rotten organizational decisions that affect EX performance. Similarly, good data will not make a jot of difference unless good decisions and actions are taken as a result. So, the triple D of data, design and decisions will need to converge a lot more intelligently and intentionally in organizations pursuing EX outcomes. Indeed, to place EX merely as a design process or function misses the point completely. Data is a natural bridge to outcomes in that it underpins and secures support for changed processes, practices and experiences. As practitioners experiment with their data and as organizations mature their EX approaches, data takes on a whole new meaning. People science actually becomes a thing and the quality of data increases as companies seek higher validity of the data they acquire and the research they do on EX. This is a good development; the starting point may well be the traditional survey and pulse approach, yet this can be the starting gun for a race to evolve data and research gathering practices. In *Employee Experience* (Whitter, 2022), I shared the return on experience (RoE) concept as a way of detailing all the valid sources of data that a company can harvest and that still applies today. Any data that helps us focus on improving experiences (operational) and improving the organization (strategic) is in scope. Inevitably, the technology that is used to supply, analyse and act on data is improving consistently year on year alongside improved methods of prioritization, which is helpful in translating company data into insight, and insight into actions that make an impact.

FIGURE 4.1 The triple D model

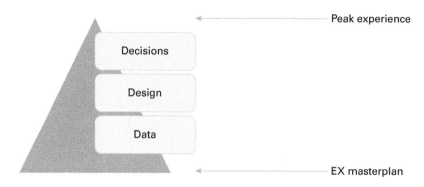

Note from Figure 4.1 that we are building up, instead of sending plans down. This is a strong point of differentiation in the way that EX leaders approach their work. As we've discussed, they dedicate an incredible amount of time to co-creation, listening and related analysis; this pays dividends at that moment and also later down the track and deep into the delivery phases.

Processes, platforms and performance

Processes: The mechanics of any experience require a certain set of actions (or inactions) to be delivered in order to create an intended outcome. A lot of the time outcomes are ill-defined and accidental, or worse, haphazard. There is an absence of a sequence of disciplined actions that increase the likelihood of success. In EX, it is perhaps one of the more important aspects of the EX masterplan; to define a set of actions that contribute a positive focus to the whole, yet support people in their moment of design and delivery. What do we want practitioners and leaders to do within their projects? What process do we want them to follow that gives a high level of autonomy and freedom, yet drives clear organizational and people outcomes?

Platforms: In advancing EX work, especially at significant scale, it quickly becomes abundantly clear that a wider platform is necessary to scaffold up and steady EX projects. In referring to platforms, this involves systems, software and products that operationalize the EX. I sort these into three categories: data, design and decisions. We can see in Figure 4.1 that the EX masterplan is broad in nature, with a wide variety of actions, activities and projects that contribute to the creation of what I could call peak experiences. As all of those elements of the blueprint come together, they start to concentrate into a narrow funnel, which ultimately crystallizes into a defined and clear outcome on the EX. This would be a peak experience. Along the way, all the data, design and decisions that take place make an immense and valuable contribution to that end targeted goal. A platform then brings all of this together.

Performance: A disciplined approach to EX means that a different set of skills and capabilities will dictate and be responsible for driving performance levels of the team, EX projects and the overall prioritized programme of work. So, the question ahead of us here is much more centred on what skills, capabilities and attributes are needed to implement and lead EX effectively on a consistent basis. If we get that sorted out, the performance will flow at both individual and team levels. If we don't bring in or develop the right capabilities then a lot of pain, frustration and unnecessary challenges await. So at this point, and as a core part of the blueprint, we'll need to consider what the ultimate EX leader/professional is.

If the HEX is the strategic map of the territory, then the 8XP framework is the blueprint to help bring good things into operation on a consistent basis. It optimizes all of those present moments to success and guides people to make their contribution. This is a wider and broader way to lead EX work, yet thinking holistically does not mean we're not thinking operationally. We're just more thoughtful about the connection points between people and their projects. Effective collaboration across functional lines doesn't come naturally to most professionals. It takes an enormous amount of dialogue and discussion to even scratch the surface of high-quality collaboration. Why is this when most colleagues are paid by the same organization to make a positive contribution? Instead, fiefdoms of expertise arise and are often positioned detrimentally to the business and the strategic plan. Alignment is hard work and this is why I position co-creation conversations as the remedy to long-standing misalignment issues, and it's incredible what can be achieved in just a few short hours.

Case in point: I was working with an EX team at one of the world's biggest companies and there was a great deal of misalignment in the very early stages of what was a short workshop. I learnt through the session that they'd never had the opportunity to come together as a team before; knowing this, I deliberately set the session up in a very open manner that challenged people to share their candid views with a high degree of transparency. It was noted through the session that they were not very aligned in the beginning; yet as we delved deeper it became obvious that alignment was not the challenge. The functional heads couldn't be more aligned if they tried as they were all focused on delivering great experiences for employees – they were just tackling this from different angles and different technical functions. The common fact was the human-centric nature of their individual approaches. This was news to them. Functional backgrounds separated them, but an overarching belief in the EX was the element that united all of them. Very quickly, the team began to form and only then could they start to realize their full potential for the benefit of the organization and its people.

From there the strength of the team grew, and suddenly, and often unexpectedly, the team started to see connection points across their functions and portfolios. One prime example was the welding of the EX to the EVP. The latter was a 12-month project rich with data that produced a strong representation of the promises being made to candidates in the market; yet up until this point it wasn't even a consideration in respect of connecting this hard-earned piece of work to the EX. That all changed when people connected the dots and realized that a strong EVP has to equal the lived experience in the organization.

SUMMARY AND ACTIONS

- Seek to unify all the core functions that impact the EX through the co-creation of a unique EX masterplan that works for your organization and context.

- Review, reflect and continue to renew the HEX through targeted strategic questions that help set the tone and foundations for the EX strategy.

- Focus on solving painful experiences for employees alongside signature work on crafting and creating your own set of peak experiences that are aligned to the brand.

- Build the experience masterplan, not experience silos. Join the dots between all the strategic themes that have emerged within the business, leverage all existing assets and resources, and lead holistically across the EX to shape work and outcomes.

- Establish a community of practice to evolve the EX, share learnings and create connections between practitioners and leaders whose roles are heavily tilted to EX. Start with those with the most significant alignment with EX and scale out.

- Work out the most valuable tools, products and services that can be utilized to underpin the work on EX strategy and enable team members to be effective with their daily practices.

- Help people meet the moment consistently by demonstrating and communicating what excellence looks like when working with your EX masterplan.

05

Experience masterplan

In previous work, I have consistently made the point that employee experience (EX) is more evolution than revolution. It starts and builds from highly effective daily practices and wise strategic leadership. In an EX sense, strategic roughly translates to holistic. We are, at all points, considering the whole organization and the whole person. Our actions and habits are formed to serve us well in that regard to ensure we fulfil our potential. Within all this strategy is the real stuff. The experiences being encountered every day and in every way. This is where true strategy lives or dies – on the frontline of the employee's everyday experience of work. There is wide scope for trial and error within this approach. To simply try something and see if it delivers. To take a risk, to be bold and courageous with our actions and to be inspired that even if perceived failure is encountered that our collective actions and endeavours will ultimately result in something impactful being delivered. This is what practitioners continue to get to grips with when it comes to EX strategy; not being right or certain all the time.

Companies worldwide have been awash with strategic leaders that are too scared to try something new. They rely on tried and trusted methods, safe bets and are often overly cautious in their approaches. It's no surprise and I don't blame them one bit. The systems and cultures around them have demanded short-term results and success, not a longer-term view based on experimental ideation. It's why the internal EX work is often significantly lagging in contrast with consumer-focused customer experience (CX) work. Yet, slowly, but surely, the shackles are being thrown out in favour of intelligent risk-taking, intrapreneurial endeavour, coupled with a bold approach to progress signature and differentiated employee experiences. Every new experience is a risk unless there is some sound strategic work behind it. In this chapter, we'll look at what the strategic foundation actually looks like. It is, in my view, the very foundation to successful strategic EX work. We are always evolving the way we do things. It needs to be this way given the speed at which expectations change. Companies have to keep up with the times and continually inspect the organizational design to ensure it is meeting and exceeding the needs of both customers and employees. This is the only way for companies to remain competitive – they must serve their people well. To navigate all the challenges and opportunities that EX brings to the fore, we'll need a masterplan.

Experience masterplan – the ingredients of EX strategy

I'd like to reflect on a few observations I've made throughout my work with companies worldwide, which will help us to think about this important part of an organization's EX strategy, and it does warrant some deeper exploration generally, given the progress being made up and down the economy with the introduction of people- and experience-based functions. For me, it comes down to several key things that need to be developed early on and continuously throughout the implementation of the EX strategy. Evidently, these will be in place across many organizations that have already embraced EX as an approach and I rarely meet a mature EX organization that doesn't have these building blocks in place in some form. A lot of hard yards goes into their production. This is the very early work that scaffolds up an anchor and guiding lights around all the work on EX. Sure, companies can launch and do well with major specific EX projects in isolation without a strong strategy behind the whole EX piece, but I find there is always that feeling that something is missing – the work is often disjointed, disconnected and quite exclusive to the people involved in its production. For that reason, success can be capped and opportunities wasted to bring something to life that has a huge, wide-ranging, and long-lasting impact. This is what good strategy can do for EX. It enhances everything and helps companies tell (and live) a more complete story that resonates with talent and prospective talent alike.

As we've discussed, alignment remains a central issue and challenge to tackle very early in EX work, and it's impossible to do this without some form of masterplan that has gone through the co-creation and feedback rounds, and then starts to resemble something that is coherent and valuable for use within the EX team and beyond into what is emerging as an EX practitioner community up, down and across the organization. The key here is giving clarity, direction and guidance to any colleague that works on EX.

FIGURE 5.1 Experience masterplan

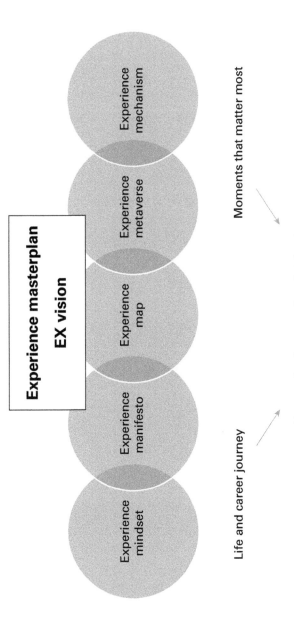

Some call this a playbook or a blueprint, but I think it is much bigger than that – it is the grand plan for EX with an associated vision for the work on EX and the approach that the organization takes.

- Experience masterplan: aligning people and the organization to the EX.
- EX vision: aligning people and the organization to a future outcome.
- Experience mindset: aligning leaders and professionals.
- Experience manifesto: aligning to the expectations of employees and the organization.
- Experience map: aligning strategic leaders and operational functions.
- Experience metaverse: aligning digital and virtual services, products and platforms.
- Experience mechanism: aligning people, projects, tools, playbooks and processes.

An evolution is just what it is. Leaders and workers are continually changing and updating the very nature of their organizations to be something that is experienced more consciously, more intentionally and more powerfully. The components will be called something different in different organizations, but the same patterns and components emerge in the process of leading and delivering EX strategy.

EX vision

Ironing out the ultimate vision for the EX is something that will need upfront investment in time and thought. It's relatively easy to spot teams and functions that run without vision. They roll from one project to another without any thought to connect anything to a desired future outcome or state. This tends to be very brand-specific and taps into related work on the employee value proposition (EVP) or consumer brand. I can't tell you how many times some great work on the overall brand has been cut off from the internal EX work and not utilized by employee-facing colleagues. It is nothing less than a travesty when it occurs and it shows the fractures, splinters and cracks in the organization. The vision then must build from within the business; no fancy consultant can come in and define the vision for you; they can help, facilitate and guide, but it has to come from within and it will really need to maximize what is already established by brand – the language, the business philosophy, the values, the viewpoints. Even if the vision is simply a core and brief statement, it will show how connected or disconnected the organization is.

A few questions to prompt thinking here would be:

- What is the overarching vision for the corporate brand?
- What language is already being communicated via the EVP?
- How do the two combine to create the vision for EX at your organization?

Reinventing the wheel here can create a new set of issues, so it is wise to draw on language that employees are already familiar with and that shows an unbreakable link to core elements of the business and related people strategies. Trying to go alone at this point by creating an entirely different piece of work can quickly establish an island for the EX and a great big sea around it. This will be no good when it is time to produce tangible business-leading results, and I do mean business-leading. Whatever the high-performing and highly regarded functions are within an organization, it is up to the EX team to place themselves in that valuable category as they scale out the EX approach. EX work has to be valuable, impactful and create a visible stir in the organization. Note it's the work that creates the stir, the experiences that are lived and delivered, and it's the unity and togetherness that is compelling as the EX strategy grows legs and moves people. That's the real impact, but it starts with vision – a bold, daring and courageous vision for what could be.

Experience mindset

Our minds manifest our experiences and create our perceptions of the world. We are constantly trying to make sense of things using our senses and the connection we have to everything that goes on around us. This can be overwhelming at times, especially at pressure or decision points. We don't need to make things any harder or more complicated than they already are – we are wonderful at doing that on our own. That's why organizations take a lead role in clarifying and simplifying things for workers and employees, and providing experiences that match up to what they need at various moments throughout the employee journey.

There's a long list of capabilities and ways of thinking that come to the fore in approaching EX as serious work. Colleagues often reshape and rebrand their skills to better showcase and story tell around their impact on EX. We can consider some of these in relation to the profile of an EX leader:

- Human-centred strategist
- Leadership enabler
- Structural engineer
- Technology shaper
- Workplace architect
- Community builder.

There is a quiet confidence that I enjoy from EX leaders. They need no external validation about the impact of their work. No awards are required to demonstrate their impact or innovation. As a group, they can often be found on the frontlines diligently making things better for employees. A well-compensated strategic executive leader hanging around the frontline? Surely not?! But yes, there is a drive about them to be immersed in, not hide from, real world problems. There is a deep satisfaction that goes alongside that. That has to be true for EX and I cannot imagine it any other way. Imagine a sales or CX person not spending time with customers. The very notion is absurd. It's just as absurd if an EX person ignores or places barriers between them and employees. I actively encourage EX leaders to go where the value is created and strategize from there, not to there. Too often strategy is thought up in corporate HQs and the frontline is the last call on a consultation journey. I've always thought that made little sense and it is still evident in some EX teams. Employees are the first, last and only defence against corporate failure; it pays to respect them and make them a firm thought within the experience mindset of teams, leaders and professionals. Yet, the more people get into EX, the more their mindset changes and appreciates the right things. It's not about us, it's about them – all employees and people within and around a business – and there is a decisive and unyielding quest to make things better, to keep on improving things.

'It's not necessarily up to us to shout from the rooftops about how clever we are, how progressive we are or how sophisticated we are. It's our place to make stuff that's as good as it can be,' said Dan Houser of Rockstar Games (*The Guardian*, 2013). This element of mindset has had a slow burn into corporate teams that have historically been lined up to govern and police employees rather than serve them and their challenges.

Experience manifesto

A core part of any EX masterplan is to define the promises that are being made to people about what they can expect and how it will be delivered in practice. These are a firm set of positions or aims that revolve around the EX work. This is important in making the step from idea to execution. What does the EX team stand for? How will they approach their work? What is top of mind in moving the EX forward?

I recall an organization I was asked to do some work with. They had notice boards in some of the corridors and I picked up a copy of their latest employee engagement action plan. There were clear items and actions listed but it was also abundantly clear that there were no aims, ideals or philosophies behind the work. It looked fragmented and disjointed because the organization and team tasked with people work were that way themselves. It was rudderless work and in total response to a poor showing on its engagement survey. Staff were, quite rightly in my view, fed up and wanted to see some tangible action on poor morale and poor management practices. Clearly, my first question to the team there was about how many of the published action points had been delivered (the leaflet was 6 months old at that point). The response didn't shock me. Nothing had been done and nothing meaningful had been delivered.

We need to take some time to set our stall out, connect our teams and philosophies, form good habits and practices, but this always starts with defining our intentions transparently within and beyond the EX team. The alignment thread runs through all of this work from idea to iteration to impact, so this is time well spent ensuring colleagues know where they stand with each other, and where they stand in the context of the organization.

Experience map

EX brings in a multi-layered and multi-functional way to squeeze out the value of every experience in a business, so why wouldn't a company line up all key employee-facing support functions to better serve the organization as a whole? The map of the organization dictates how strategy is delivered in practice and goes a long way to create the prevailing attitude and atmosphere across the EX. Support functions, and those in service to people, should surely lead by example in EX, and this might well require radical change at the centre of the business structure.

It's not really radical though, it is simply a case of repositioning and realigning any disconnected services to ensure cross-functional collaboration drives quick and tangible gains for the company. A map, for example, can be naturally bigger than the roles and formal responsibilities that have been assigned. Since EX reaches deep into a company, so must we to find positive outcomes. In reality, this means our work and our approach will influence people beyond our formal authority. There is no choice for businesses but to move people and teams in a certain direction that is more favourable for EX to be applied effectively.

The interesting thing about defining and bringing the experience map to life is that all the varied and rich work going on will come to the surface of the organization. There will be teams, leaders and colleagues doing some amazing work on EX, though it will be under the radar, but working well in plain sight. Building an experience map provides a level of clarity to help strategic leaders make better decisions with better data and input from colleagues, and with more refined long-term and connected intentions. It always amuses me when a kind of mind map emerges that highlights all of the functions and people that touch the EX. Then the realization often dawns that none of these colleagues have ever spoken to each other, especially across complex multinational corporations, yet they are all working on and impacting the same thing – the experience of work. This revelation then merges with another – the EX team is bigger than we first thought! Yes, the map does tend to start small, with a very small handful of colleagues at the centre of the company formally defined as working on EX. Yet this idea quickly changes when bringing the experience map into play – marketing, estates, HR, IT, communication, facilities and so on – all will be working on EX in some form, and I would think of these colleagues as part of the wider EX team, and that's just the formal roles. The EX ecosystem is enriched by groups, committees, partners, vendors, suppliers and other interested parties. The map grows and so too does the territory for EX operations, activities and related communications. This, practically, takes the idea that EX is a collective organization-wide idea and turns it into something visually representative and powerful.

Experience metaverse

For this book, and in the context of EX, I look at the metaverse as an exciting potential prospect within companies where employees spend their digital work lives, and increasingly, virtual reality (VR) and augmented reality will help facilitate that and will be evident in a wide range of employee-related programmes. The digital world is already upon us. Many workers had their first real taste of digital, remote and virtual work through the pandemic. In any case, the world is not going back to the way things were pre-pandemic. Opportunities to develop careers and impact in hybrid ways has, no doubt, been the biggest aspect of working life in recent years. Like anything, some have gone all-in on this new way of doing things, while some are looking to claw back virtual and home-working privileges and pretend the new work styles didn't emerge at all. Others are caught in-between and are treading a fine line between what companies would like as the standard work operating model and the increased expectations from employees about flexible work. Several elements of flexible work have been hard won, but the ability to run work and schedules remotely was handed to employees on a plate during the pandemic. It enables businesses to continue to exist, and many to thrive and experience surges in productivity. The metaverse was already on its way, but the pandemic has greatly accelerated adoption and awareness amongst companies. It is, if predictions are accurate, the next frontier of work life.

The metaverse, while certainly a step beyond the current digital employee experience, will be the next step in creating an immersive internal world built on virtual reality and the latest technologies that combine to create digital places and spaces where people can get things done and interact in different ways. There is the obvious gold rush from a consumer perspective for companies to lead and influence the metaverse on the outside of their business, but internally, the term does bring together many of the emerging elements of the digital EX and what companies have been hoping to deliver inside their businesses – a seamless, integrated and connected digital place where employees can be productive (and increasingly, even more productive) by utilizing their company's virtual world complete with their own avatars, holograms or virtual self.

'I think the Metaverse is the all-encompassing space in which all digital experience sits; the observable digital universe made up of millions of digital galaxies,' said Eric Redmond who is the Global Director, Technology Innovation, Nike (Hackl, 2021). How this digital life emerges remains to be seen, and also the questions over whether people really want to bring their entire digital lives into one place; yet employers are starting to look at the digital life of their employees and how it applies in their context, and it's a wise thing to do. In fact, the catalyst to create much broader and more widely mandated EX strategies can often be some good early work on the digital experience at work. Think of the head start that the early adopters of the internet had and how that profoundly shaped the future of their business. What I'm clear on though is the idea that the digital world from an employee perspective needs to adapt to advancing technologies and be as integrated and seamless as possible across the EX to help people access information, communicate and connect with colleagues in high-impact ways, and to fully utilize the online world to solve problems and respond to opportunities across EX projects. It is strategically important to ensure our digital worlds are in order and enhancing the overall EX, so it makes a lot of sense to get on the front foot with this.

There's been a lot of introspection about technology in the workplace. HR and EX technology has exploded and integration continues to be key to remove any residual feeling of clunkiness and bureaucracy in the technology being used within EX. A metaverse is a logical next step in technology adoption for organizations, and if fully harnessed, will transform the EX completely and also the way people carry out their tasks and run their work lives. It's an exciting time that is being met with a healthy dose of cynical interrogation, but people can't really argue with what is already there.

Over 1,500 employees and 1,500 companies in the US were surveyed by ExpressVPN and the reported statistics are interesting in that they capture the changing attitudes of employees in relation to the metaverse (ExpressVPN, 2022). Once the reserve of sci-fi aficionados, the metaverse is starting to create new career choices and new expectations in work practices. The findings of the survey indicated that the metaverse was appealing as a way to work due to:

- increased work-from-home flexibility (45 per cent)
- an easier way to collaborate with co-workers (36 per cent)
- increased job opportunities (33 per cent)
- ability to 'travel' virtually (33 per cent).

It's not all rosy though and thankfully so given the over-reaching of some employers to over-monitor their workforces; employer surveillance was the top concern cited by respondents alongside digital privacy and security. So, companies will need to think about this within experience architecture and the masterplan, and move sensitively in how they build out their digital worlds. Technology is effective when used to connect people in a positive way. The danger is going too far and too fast strategically with an approach that employees neither want nor would tolerate.

Experience mechanism

Companies want results with EX. No ifs or buts, just outcomes. They want EX to attract and retain the talent they need to deliver superior year-on-year growth, productivity and business performance. It's not a difficult equation to understand. It can be a challenging equation to deliver though without the right mechanisms in place to replicate results and bring in a more consistent approach to EX across the entire organization. They can achieve this through selecting the right tools, refining the processes that lead to peak and powerful experiences, and setting a natural standard for all EX projects. For me, this is the final piece in the jigsaw. Organizations can travel down blind alleys unless they have developed the right mindsets, the right map, the right manifesto, the right metaverse – and across all of those things there will be clear differences between teams, functions and colleagues. This does not help the EX work or any EX projects. The key here is to unify these big things first and then start to understand what tools, what techniques and what practices can be used to design or redesign strong, positive experiences on a more consistent basis across the organization. Actions and reactions dictate how well an experience can be brought into play – a coherent process that can be used across different teams and departments with specialist support built in is worth its weight in gold when bringing all manner of experiences to life. I discuss this more specifically when exploring the EX ecosystem, but here companies start to lay out things like design thinking, human-centred design, agile methodologies, employee journey mapping, personal development and many other resources that are lined up to drive stronger outcomes and a more consistent approach to EX within a company.

A prime part of the mechanism will be the holistic employee experience (HEX) as a tool to navigate the employee experience holistically at the outset of any projects. It complements and is a key overarching element that sits across a range of processes including design thinking, and keeps the core areas of EX consistently top of mind within projects and decision points.

The life and career journey

The human experience has come to the fore within EX in recent years, and will remain a key area of concern within the EX strategy. Any EX strategy being shaped to focus simply on an employee's life in work will fall short. Indeed, the experience that people have in life more generally is the key to a successful EX strategy. An end-to-end focus on the journeys that people have in life and work has crept into and beyond the work of HR functions.

The more colleagues view employment as a journey, the better. It is very helpful when considering all the projects and plays that are scoped out to enhance and enrich the experience of work. Viewing things as a journey is also a reliable way to identify issues between functions, teams and services. Issues emerge perhaps from one point in the journey to the other. The role of the EX leader is to help the organization navigate and transform these issues into small victories for the business. Small victories stack up into bigger long-term wins, and there are plenty to be found across the employee journey once we start looking for them. This could be simplifying processes, tools or systems that employees interact with, or it could be wholesale changes in how the organization leads EX. Many have adopted new themes, new functions and new roles to achieve this, as mentioned, and I predict that this will continue to snowball as some serious cross-fertilization of ideas, skills and knowledge permeate all the support functions that an organization stands up to serve people. A clunky and cumbersome journey is often made by clunky and cumbersome support functions that lack vision, connection and vibrancy.

Moments that matter most

An absolutely critical understanding has emerged amongst EX professionals. Not all moments are created equal. If we think about the critical moments that employees experience in their life and career journey, some matter a whole lot more than others. These are very familiar to you and very familiar to the rest of us. They matter. It makes complete sense to lean the EX strategy into them fully to create a bridge between the organization and its people. Not being led by policies, but crafting experiences around these pivotal human moments. Good organizations do this well, great organizations do this consistently well.

What type of moments are we talking about?

The life bingo card in Table 5.1 is illustrative and not exhaustive, of course. Some of the events and milestones we can conveniently and neatly place on the employee journey with a high degree of certainty that those things will happen and come to pass for each individual, but others are subject to life bingo and are quite random in how and when they occur. Some can be planned, but many elements of life can be quite unexpected.

TABLE 5.1 The life bingo card

Job appointment day	Birthday	Holidays	Social justice and planet-focused events	Creative events and pursuits (passion projects)
First day/week/ month/year	Paternity	Sabbaticals	Mental health and well-being challenges	Retirement, redundancy, redeployment
Major work victories	House move	Belief-based leave events	Personal crisis points	Boomerang and contingent experiences
Team meetings & 1:1s	Marriage/ wedding and partnerships	Significant national events	Significant national challenges (cost of living, energy, environment, war)	Promotion and career transitions (lateral, upward, downward, outward)
Sickness and absence events (for employee and others)	Birth of loved one or adopting a family member	Cultural events and milestones	Unexpected life changes, challenges, and opportunities	Evolving as parents, grandparents and carers

That doesn't mean we can't strategize for them though. We can prepare our responses to extreme cases, and drive into the business a human-centred and experience-driven philosophy that meets the moment. Out of all these moments, and as part of a good strategy, we'll need to determine the moments that matter most to people. The ones that need that special attention to detail – the ones that can make or break the employment relationship. It is here we find an organization's unique strengths and where organizational culture faces its sternest test. In strategic terms, I'd want to know in real time or as close to real time as possible, what moments are of most concern to employees. They may change, but some will stubbornly remain the same, so powerful an impact they have on emotions. The one I keep coming back to in my coaching and speaking is personal crisis points – this is a large category and there are many things in life that will crop up to create challenges for people. This could be physical, emotional, financial or spiritual. They could be affecting the person or it could be related to their family or loved ones. It is at these moments that the relationship with employees grows or declines. Is the EX positioned to strongly support people through their testing moments?

Are leaders enabled to lead through these sorts of tough moments? Have the right mechanisms and infrastructure been developed and deployed to shape a supportive response?

I can almost guarantee that colleagues looking over the life bingo card will identify some moments that are not quite as they should be, and deserve a second look and further investment. This is not so unusual given the wide range of moments that sit in different functions and under different stewards. Putting in place a masterplan will start to draw out the moments and milestones that could be getting away. There is also a pressure on strategic leaders to deal in strategic things – the big and expensive projects and end-to-end journeys; yet we'll need to be careful that we're spending time on things that matter most to employees, not just the organization. This is where EX strategy really makes the difference it should.

SUMMARY

Starting to think about the experience masterplan is a good step to take to get the EX strategy off the ground and into motion. I wouldn't delay this. Yes, the temptation and pressure will continue to focus on the good old low-hanging fruit and all quick wins, but it will serve you well to take a large step back to look at the overall masterplan for your organization, its people and the experiences they have. In reality, the experience masterplan and the experience ecosystem will be developing simultaneously as EX leaders move around and explore their organizations with this fresh human-centred perspective, and that's a good thing. This work will evolve and you will evolve with it.

- Reflect on your experience masterplan and all of its constituent parts. Are you building a connected, coherent and compelling EX strategy?

- Consider how each part of the masterplan is shaping up for your organization and EX team. Are you missing anything? Is there more work to do? Get onto it now rather than later.

- Delve into your existing employee journey and review moment performance, especially those milestones in life and work deemed to be critical moments by employees in your context.

- Map all of the functions and roles that interact with, are responsible for and determine EX outcomes. Keep building the map as we begin our work on the EX ecosystem.

06

Team performance – a recipe for employee experience success

A strong EX strategy quickly becomes part of the lived and loved experience within an organization. Of course, it starts with the first leader, the first followers and the first sponsors and supporters, but it has a habit of taking on a life of its own once the foundations are fully in place. In this chapter, we delve a bit more thoroughly into the team behind the strategy and people driving the experience movement within an organization. I feel it's important to highlight several key areas in what makes an employee experience (EX) team successful in practice. I have observed many EX teams at close quarters over the years and have drawn out a number of ingredients that separate the best from the rest. By best, I mean they have a consistent, visible and sustained impact on EX performance holistically. A team has formed, often in the early stages of EX strategy development, and it has not only stayed together, but unbreakable bonds have been forged in the fires of co-creation and redesigning the experience of the company.

Experiencing team performance

Team performance is a primary concern when working on EX strategy and it needs to be from the outset of any project. It is remarkable how little I hear about EX performance – how all the respective parts of the EX are performing as a whole and also with regard to the intentions a business has around EX performance. This is a developing area as companies begin to mature their measurement approaches and start to connect the dots across functions to tell a more absorbing one-brand story.

But performance should be considered by the EX team (in whatever form that EX team takes) at the outset of any work on strategy. I'm not talking about research studies on EX by Harvard and the like. There is a high-quality and highly valid body of research that demonstrates the positive impact of EX on business performance. What I'm talking about now is more specific in relation to the performance of the EX holistically, and I'll dive into this in more depth in the next chapter. What is clear is that a total picture of EX performance only emerges once the EX team has started to form and take shape. All of the different facets of the EX come into focus and then we can begin identifying what data and measures are already in place that help us tell the story of EX more coherently and consistently to internal and external audiences. But the performance of EX needs to move to the centre of the conversation.

- How is the EX performing?
- How is the EX team performing?
- How are individuals within the EX team performing?
- How is the business being impacted by EX performance?

Yes, performance and employee experience would do well to stay together as we develop strategy and the team associated with its delivery. Once we start to get really good at discussing EX performance, we can then mature that into the discussion about its impact on business performances across the business. It's still not a common expression though. EX performance is usually anchored or expressed in terms of survey data, most likely engagement data, and that is so limited in scope and depth, and it doesn't do justice to all the work that goes on across the EX holistically – across the community, the technology, the structure, the workplace, the leadership system and the work to bring more humanity into everyday business practices.

It's for that reason I bring performance to the top of this chapter before even starting the dialogue about the EX team. We must get used to talking about EX in performance terms backed with data, evidence and clear examples, as this will enable the team to drive real and significant business conversations while at the same time more closely connecting EX to the fortunes of the company. It's a good discussion to have as there's not a minute wasted talking about EX performance – this is research that feeds our co-creation machine and the EX team is going to be at the centre of all that too. With the EX team though, we'll need to revisit our ideas on what a team is. A team is usually, certainly in the corporate world, viewed to be colleagues who work in the same functional area or specialism – they are situated in the same structure and usually have the same manager. In EX strategy terms, the team is an expanded idea that crosses functions, roles and responsibilities. It is not defined by structural titles or positions. Indeed, it is often defined by the amount of impact and influence a role or colleague has over the EX as a result of their role characteristic and the type of work that they do. EX blurs corporate boundaries, and for good reason given that EX has a vast array of touchpoints that rest within a wide range of business support and leadership functions. The good news is that EX has already borne many excellent trailblazers who leave signposts along the way to further support those just starting or seeking to improve their EX strategies and team development. So, how do we get a team moving in the right direction from the outset? What are the practices and elements that have already helped strong-performing EX teams deliver?

Getting the philosophy right

In practice, the elements that I've observed tend not to be high-level intellectual concepts, but practical and pragmatic themes that generate positive actions, commitments and movements. They combine to shape an organization's approach to EX in a sustainable and high-energy manner. What is interesting about this is the starting point. Teams working on EX come together and really have to start their careers again. Colleagues challenge their belief systems and the very foundation on which an organization is built. From management-centred to people-centred is no easy step when it comes to mindset and team formation.

We have to remember that people serve different masters within organizations and agendas may not be well aligned throughout daily and more strategic practices. Silos and functional fiefdoms are the evidence of this. They are an outcome of misalignment and a poor holistic team. Centres of excellence can feel like this too – the company has set up these specialist centres to deepen and accelerate progress, yet if the islands are not connected strongly then performance levels are capped and limited to areas of expertise. If a company chooses to build these islands, at least build some bridges between them! This is where EX strategy can be pivotal or even a sea change in how organizations operate because we begin to question everything and everyone that stands in between the organization and the people. Indeed, the organization is the people, so human centricity must run through every aspect of our work. I am fairly black and white on this point. There is no grey area here. A valuable company is created by valued employees and workers, so all functions need to rally around people.

We've discussed this earlier in relation to the mindset of practitioners and leaders working on EX projects, and it is equally important to consider the team and how it interacts over the long term. But is membership exclusive, and what do we mean by team in the context of EX strategy?

A team approach – co-leading the employee experience strategy

At a strategic level, the team usually begins with those very first appointments into formal EX roles. We see a range of job titles around this, including chief EX officer, EX managers, global EX partner, vice president (VP) EX, and so on. The title is a signal to the business that something is happening, yet it is, of course, the substance that matters. What changes, what improves, and what makes people (and the organization) more whole. There has to be some care in how and when the team is brought together. It is not unusual for those charged with EX strategy to take their time exploring the organization, mind mapping all the functions and individuals involved in EX, and seeking out some of the early strategic barriers and opportunities to get things moving. Is it better to form a team when there is at least some momentum behind the overall EX work, or do you bring people in cold and co-create from there? The best answer and one that I advise on professionally is somewhere in the middle. The proof of concept will still need to be managed, sponsors will need to be satisfied that progress is happening, and the CEO will want to see tangible and swift actions taking place. Results will need to be evidenced.

What does this look like in practice? Well, a couple of company-wide projects usually fall into development scope – they are often areas that have been ripe for improvement for some time, like the onboarding experience as an example. Investment will be required, systems and processes will be upgraded, and the overall journey will be redesigned from start to finish. What better way to bring a cross-functional squad or team together than to work on something very meaningful and significant for employees? This is the reality – real projects will start to establish the team in any case, but we can also start putting in place longer-term intentions around how the right roles and people can combine to drive consistently high-quality EX performance.

Beyond the formal EX roles, we know that there are many EX leaders operating across the organizational landscape – IT/digital, marketing, campus and estates, communications and branding, and many more besides. All of these functional roles, and the related portfolio of projects, will be unleashing a wide range of outcomes (positive and negative) on the workforce every day. It is important to bring these colleagues into the fold, as mentioned, via real projects while simultaneously cultivating relationships that will strengthen the EX team membership.

Some members of the EX team will make total sense when looking at the organization chart, yet others may not. This has been an intriguing development in EX; in driving EX strategy there is often a view taken that informal influence as well as formal influence should be accounted for in the overall membership of the EX team. Yes, in the main, we would want people in the team that have functional control and responsibility, but there will be some people within the organization – those with significant influence amongst employees and managers – that it makes total sense to have onboard in a more formal way. Why limit their role to champion or change agent or those other corporate clichés? If people can make a significant contribution in landing and sustaining a high-performing EX strategy, I'd prefer it that they were on the team and committed to the EX mission.

This is another important aspect of EX to mention in that it has shifted thinking around what a team is and how it comes together in the first place. Working on the employee experience in a holistic way leaves us with little choice in this regard. Our scorecard is entirely dependent on how well we work with our peers and how strong that feeling of team really is. A human resource director (HRD) working with an IT director to elevate the digital EX is a helpful reference point that springs to mind, given that those roles and their teams will criss-cross each other on so many touchpoints. Now, traditionally, these functions and many others will focus on their own domains and very rarely develop any sense of team, and if they do, it is often short-lived. If the strategic leaders can't get their act together then there is little hope for their teams either.

Planning for high employee experience performance

Strong team performance is no happy accident. It is created intentionally. I'll start to draw out some of the priority areas to concentrate efforts. These ideas have emerged because they have worked in practice for EX teams. As you'll see, there's no fluffy stuff to be found. It's just real actionable and tangible things that are very helpful in standing up a wider EX team and helping them to perform as a team over a sustained period of time. Our aim here is to build a new way of working between functions and eliminate any sign of silo behaviours or thinking. That's because a holistic approach to EX is hard work, and it will be harder if things and teams are not joined up, operating from different playbooks, or nowhere near the same page. But where does it all start?

Six unbreakable laws of a successful EX team

After many years of observations based on working directly with the world's first EX teams and many of those that have followed them since, it has become abundantly clear that not all teams are created equal. There are major differences in roles, in the investment levels and in the overall positioning (and backing) of the team (and broader cross-functional EX team) in the structure. For many, as discussed, it starts with a small number of formal strategic roles to get things moving and the wise EX leader starts almost immediately to broaden the approach and expand the team informally, and formally where possible, with some form of cross-functional group emerging out of that.

Regardless of the context, any EX team will fail if they break the laws I'm about to present. Irrespective of the resources a team is afforded, if these basic ingredients are not part of the mix, then the scope of the team's impact will be severely limited. Good work can emerge, but in the cold light of day, it may not be great work, and I suspect great work and great performance has to be an intended outcome when bringing a group of people together. It's also an inspiring journey to high performance, finding limits and breaking them, and doing it with a strong sense of togetherness knowing that if that team didn't exist, the EX would be much, much weaker for it. So, these laws are guardrails in the formation and development of the team at the centre of the EX work, and I recommend we follow them wisely and with care.

BE TRANSPARENT

As a strategic EX leader, vulnerability, especially with peers and employees, is nothing to be feared; if it is, then we really do need to expedite the work on the culture of the organization. Failing that, be the change you wish to see is a sensible idea. I often walked into organizations in a turnaround situation armed only with a blank piece of paper, intent on co-creating solutions to major organizational challenges. When I observe EX leaders doing this as a practice, it is not weakness, but strategic sense. There is no real point in prioritizing problems that employees are not concerned about and there is little point in creating false platforms based on false promises and unrealistic expectations. These things tend to fracture the employment relationship beyond repair.

This is why I advocate for transparency in EX work. Whether building the team or co-creating at a deeper level with employees, being upfront and honest about the context and its challenges serves as a rallying cry to attract positive and like-minded people to the cause. An overly corporate and stage-managed approach can weaken things – I enjoy seeing employees solve their own problems and co-create their own experiences, and then reflect on the outcomes. It is the people that will drive the EX forward and it starts with the team. Being transparent strips out the ego and levels the playing field considerably.

As a strategic EX leader, the burden to take everything on and fix every problem is something that requires management unless burnout is a desirable outcome. I've been there and done that, but what helped me run projects and teams was a commitment to sharing the challenges, sharing data, sharing knowledge and being absolutely clear about where we are and where we want to be. Yes, this can escalate very positively because openness and togetherness does heighten ambition, so we also have to be upfront about and gauge where the team's vision is going. Being average is not exciting and will do little to form a high-performing team, yet the energy for a bigger industry-leading mission has to develop from within the team and with the support of positive leadership. If the team want to raise their game and become the best at what they do, that's great and should be encouraged, but all of the usual concerns must be aired and an optimistic realism instilled into the team by default.

Leading the team with transparency at the core and being intentional about how colleagues connect and interact with each other makes everything else all the more comfortable. Real relationships, cultivated across functions, is a very good outcome of the EX strategy. The added bonus is that transparency is like rocket fuel when it comes to building trust.

BUILD TRUST

At the heart of any EX strategy and team is trust. It's an outcome of the shared experiences we co-create across the strategic masterplan for EX. Shared experiences help build and maintain trust, and we ought to be very careful about the communications practices we initiate within the team. Take a moment to consider the situation. We're working on an EX strategy that involves many different functions, not just HR. For years, there have been major disconnects with the work of these functions. Aside from a well-managed committee or executive group, many of the functional heads will simply revert to their own individual objectives to prove their value and get things done. Why? Because collaboration is not easy and it can naturally slow things down if solid relationships have not been built beforehand. There's a lack of trust that pervades these relationships and getting the simplest of things done becomes a jarring experience. I'm sure that you've had experiences like this, but putting in the work on the cross-functional EX team and guiding people to deliver trust-building actions is a major element of team success. So, how do we do that?

This is where the strategic EX leader earns their money because they make all the difference here in creating an atmosphere around the EX work. We will feel welcome, respected, safe, encouraged, supported, and we move forward projects and priorities in a positive, optimistic and pragmatic way, acknowledging that a lot of learning will take place, and that only makes the team (and the EX strategy) stronger. There will be also be consistency in the practicalities of team management: regular meetings, open communication, shared workspaces, shared objectives and an unyielding focus on delivering high-quality experiences in work. To be surrounded by people on the same mission develops trust, but real and genuine alignment is key to the whole thing.

BE ALIGNED AND ACCOUNTABLE

The greatest challenge of the EX era is this one. How do you bring functions and people together and unify them around delivering high EX performance? It's a question many organizations are failing to even consider at the outset of the EX work. In all of my experiences with companies around the world, I can easily identify problems in EX strategy work, and a lot of them stem from a lack of alignment and accountability. In bringing a cross-function EX team together, there'll need to be some introspection and reflection about how well the current structure is serving the EX. Ideally, we can change it, but that is not often possible. Instead, we'll need to co-create a team leadership approach that both aligns functional heads and their teams on EX projects, and holds them to account for outcomes. The exact shape of this will look and be experienced differently based on the methodologies and culture of each unique organization, yet they will all be trying to reach the same outcome: an aligned, effective and high-performing team.

Often, it is difficult to figure out what is going on in functions that are not our own and they move very differently, so aligning people and bringing them into the EX fold quickly is, for me, a firm priority in team development. As we discussed earlier, the philosophy of the team is fundamental – how people think about employees and how they relate to them and the organization is really quite important. This is why figuring out a way to measure contribution at individual, team and organizational levels is going to be something that the team needs to explore in the early stages.

MAINTAIN A STABLE CORE
The core as I term it here is the engine room of the team. There will be a few central players who strategically have the mandate to accelerate, guide and maintain the corporate focus on EX. Colleagues in these roles are seriously integral to the success of the EX strategy. They will bring a stability (and enduring momentum) to the overall programme as the pace gathers, especially as we reflect on all the projects and the work that touches the holistic employee experience (HEX). Many projects contribute to the overall health of the HEX and will make their contribution to it. I have to say in some teams, a core of colleagues become the magnet for great things and experiences, and can rapidly advance the EX strategy. It is also a support network of colleagues who should be aligned and working for the good of the company anyway, and also reflective and role models of the values that a company espouses. The proof is in the pudding – the EX work is the pudding. Just how strong and effective these relationships will be is discovered in the roll-out of the EX strategy.

The core of the team is also vital in sharing intelligence, connecting the dots between functional projects that impact the EX, and also ensuring sponsors on the executive team remain fully engaged and briefed in the EX work from all sides and all angles of the organization. If you're a senior leader sitting on a management team, and you keep hearing about EX through the lens of different, but aligned colleagues and functions, the message will not go unheard, and this is also helpful in crafting the strategic communication narrative. The employer brand is the marketing, the employee experience is the reality – the core can help the brand and the EX reflect each other, and tell a more unified story to attract, retain and encourage a high-performing workforce.

CELEBRATE MOMENTS AND MILESTONES
Again, this law is not some abstract idea that cannot be applied. What I've learned from observing and working with the very best EX teams is that

they are constantly moving from one milestone to another. One building from the next, bringing order and consistency to the EX in more ways than one. It's refreshing to see the emphasis being placed on EX innovation and improvement, with recognition and respect being placed on each development. High quality should be celebrated, and it is also a platform to build for future success. It generates good feelings and serves as a reference point for the organization to look up to and explore more within different teams. So many times, it is the simple things that break through and change things for the better. Our example is far more important than we realize, but it has ramifications beyond the boundaries of our responsibilities.

Too often, there is not enough attention placed on recognizing and respecting cross-functional endeavours that serve the greater good of the organization. Indeed, in the experience economy, those colleagues who lead and embrace this new powerful style of co-creation across functions will be in the zenith and of high value in the talent marketplace. Drawing people together to work on EX is one thing; keeping them together and performing well despite an organization design that often prevents great collaboration from occurring in the first place is solid EX leadership and should be commended and learnt from wherever it happens. There is something bonding about co-creating the overall EX strategy and EX priorities, and then going through and delivering against them in partnership with colleagues and employees alike. We have to remember at all times that the team scaffolding an approach to EX is having an experience too – it will need to be a good one!

ENJOY THE EXPERIENCE

This is a law in any work that I'm involved with, and great EX teams around the world seemingly apply this law automatically. For me, it goes deeper. This is a life philosophy and a rather useful and excellent measure of success: are we enjoying the experience?

Enjoyment is not often mentioned as a measure of team success, but I think perhaps it should be for various reasons. Things have become harder and more challenging in the EX world. A pandemic and post-pandemic world of work to design and roll out in record time, wars, energy crises, and on top of all that, a general cost-of-living crisis and greater economic uncertainty. There's a lot going on in the world that can quickly sour the mood. Leading and managing projects and strategies inevitably means we'll have to deal with expected and unexpected challenges if we are to fulfil our potential and exceed our objectives. Whether internal or external, these challenges will demand some form of response. Yet, if you give two leaders the same challenges and one was determined to enjoy the experience come what may, I can confidently say which team I would elect to be in. The point here is that EX teams are often incubated in the midst of great challenges, but what is significant is the enjoyment they derive from their work despite all the challenges and barriers against them. They truly enjoy the experience of solving problems, fixing things and maximizing opportunities to expand and extend the impact and outcomes associated with EX.

In this sense, the team will be at its best when it enjoys working together. It's not painful. It's not awkward. It's enjoyable despite any challenges that present. I do think this should be considered as a wider foundation stone in team development. When people reflect on their lived experience, it is this point that quickly comes to the fore. They cite times of challenge and enjoyment, and they often occurred at the same time. Questions to keep in mind as the EX team forms is:

- Is the team enjoying its work and enjoying the experience of working together?
- If not, what needs to change? How can we co-create a more enjoyable team experience?
- What's getting in the way of positive relationships between team members?

Asking these questions may well surface a few issues getting in the way of powerful co-creation. It could be that the systems, practices, tools, platforms and processes need some revamping, or there may be other things coming into play that will need some solutions, but in any case, we go back to co-creation to generate the kind of team experience that is enjoyable to be part of, and this, in turn, develops a pathway to even higher team performance.

A powerful accelerator for EX success

Getting the team right, the dynamics right, the practices right and the working rhythms right goes a long way to cementing a unified and holistic approach to EX for any organization. If only more time was invested in this from the outset, a lot of EX opportunities could be realized much sooner. Usually, the inevitable penny drops when a company has embarked on one or two projects designed to improve the EX. They go through this process and realize how weakly connected their functions and teams are. It becomes a massive pain point just to get equipment ready for an employee's first day, or to coordinate seemingly simple events or transitions along the employee journey, or technology doesn't connect across functions and employees get confused or lost in the system. All of those outcomes are reflective of an organization that is not set up adequately to deal with the EX holistically and its approach that organizations surely don't want to maintain and keep replicating. Yet, so many have to go through the pain themselves in order to make the required changes. They have to find out directly that collaboration across functional boundaries is hard, that easy tasks are not so easy, and that communication is too complex between colleagues and teams.

While it is valuable for organizations and their bureaucracies to experience such pain, I'd rather they avoided it in the first place, or at the very least minimized it, because it slows progress and the employee experience will suffer as a result. Good intentions are simply not enough and the system may well resist any change to it if a lone wolf EX leader comes knocking with their fancy new ideas about treating people as human beings and making every moment and experience count within the organization. One lone colleague with good intentions and even better ideas will easily be defeated by a well-established system that is resistant to any form of change. But what if it was the system that was changing itself? That's what we're doing here with EX. We're changing the system of management and leadership from the inside. Building a cross-functional EX team ensures that all parts of the whole support system infrastructure and all the related services are represented and aligned with the changes to come – indeed, they are driving the changes themselves directly.

Make no mistake, EX changes the way you see things, it changes what you work on, and it changes the way you work with each other. This is only a good thing for the organization, which is merely a vehicle for an idea, a purpose and a mission that is delivered in full by people. If we are to truly and sustainably affect EX performance, we'll need to get our house in order first by exemplifying many of the things that we've discussed in this chapter.

SUMMARY

- For consistent and exceptional EX team performance, we'll need to reconfigure our views about what a team actually is and how it develops beyond functional boundaries.

- Review the unbreakable laws of EX team success. How is your EX team performance stacking up?

- Consider the scale and depth of your EX strategy. Are your bases covered? Do you have the right combination of skills, capabilities and attributes that will sustain an organization-wide and holistic EX?

- Consider how the EX team can become more aligned and more accountable for EX performance, and how high-value impact can be a visible and constant theme within the EX approach.

07

Driving holistic employee experience performance

At the initial stages of a company's journey into the employee experience, a lot of emphasis is placed on raising awareness, education and the search for quick wins around the organization. Things that stand out as needing some immediate care and attention when looking at them through the lens of experience. Employee experience (EX) does change the way we approach our work in all different kinds of ways, but the primary one is the shift to a much more committed form of human-centred leadership across a business – this is exemplified by the very practical and powerful focus on EX. In this chapter, we'll explore the holistic employee experience (HEX) in performance terms, drawing out some significant themes that require more consideration while seeking to overcome new and unexpected challenges that have presented themselves around the economy. Many of these global events and challenges are outside of our immediate control, yet the HEX remains firmly within our control and under our direct influence as companies. We can make a significant contribution to our organization by driving key performance outcomes through every element of the HEX. We started with awareness, and now it's much more about everyday performance.

In *Employee Experience* (Whitter, 2022), I sought to establish a major strategic reference point, lens and tool to guide practitioners in advancing the EX at their businesses. The HEX has been taken up by many global organizations now and is a central part of their EX strategies. The world is filled with so many organizations though and many are still trailing well behind the EX frontrunners.

From awareness to performance

It's one thing to be aware of something, it's a different matter entirely to take actions and generate strong performance returns based on a new approach to business, which EX clearly is. The focus on EX as an implementable and scalable business idea has been massively advanced by necessity during and after the pandemic. Organizations have been challenged like never before to build an EX that complements and integrates well with the human experience. These new work configurations are being tested to the max in recent times with mass layoffs, busy strike seasons and a growing resentment generally towards working conditions and pay settlements. Companies now have the stick or twist moment to deal with too; flexibility has been a key carrot being dangled by companies to entice candidates into their organizations – this is a demand and supply issue as workers have expressed flexibility as a consistent top priority, and employers during the pandemic have been more than happy to accommodate and encourage that.

Fast forward to the present day and it's a different story, with no clear consensus on which configuration of work will rise above the rest and become the 'norm' or business standard. Performance then has become somewhat a subjective discourse across executive teams. Despite evidence emerging during the pandemic that workers are more productive, healthier and happier, corporate HQs are beginning to move in a different direction by demanding a return to the office. The narrative around this tends to pitch management against workers, but I still feel the context and co-creation are key to decisions of this kind, and there is a need for a clear alignment between people and the company. The large and global round of mass layoffs will be an interesting period and litmus test when it comes to talent decisions. There might be fewer options available in the system with the flexibility that candidates would want to see, and businesses may also struggle to attract their first-choice candidates if flexibility is no longer a key part of the EX. The thing to remember here is that in any scenario, any labour market or economic challenge or period of uncertainty, talented people always have choices.

For this and many other reasons, companies and colleagues will need to raise their game when it comes to harnessing the full performance potential of the HEX. Every element has been impacted by global events, and we'll need to double down and start to look at each element much more carefully in terms of tangible performance outcomes. I have highlighted the return on experience (RoE) previously and that encompasses a large body of potential outcomes across the HEX that help to tell a one-brand story – a story that ends with a company being admired, respected and trusted, not just in the talent marketplace, but in society at large.

The times change, the HEX changes with them though. The real area of concern for me when reflecting on overall HEX performance is strength, unity and health. This surfaces some really core strategic questions about the elements of the HEX that we need to consider over and over again come what may.

Looking out and across all the HEX performance elements, we can consider the following questions.

STRENGTH

- Is there a strong connection to the organizational Truth (purpose, mission and values)?
- Are the connections and relationships between each of the elements strong?

HEALTH

- Is the organization healthy?
- Are people within the organization healthy?

UNITY

- Are people aligned to the needs of the business?
- Is the organization aligned to the needs of the people?

I have run people through straightforward HEX assessments many times. Strategically, we can quickly understand and grasp how a company is performing across all the respective parts of the EX. Companies know if leadership quality and performance is at a good level. Companies know if technology is serving them well. Companies know if a community is vibrant or not. It is then not difficult to arrive at a pretty accurate picture of HEX performance which will be backed up by qualitative and quantitative data in abundance from across the whole organizational ecosystem. After many years in the field, surveys and data points serve to validate what we already know to be true. Why? Because we live and experience it daily. We know what is what within the organization. Of course, data points are insightful and impactful, helping us to target priorities and improvements where they count and get valuable insights for business cases.

So, what is happening across the HEX elements today and what do we need to prioritize in terms of EX strategy? Let's move forward and explore this.

Human performance

The human element of the HEX has always been about working with employees as co-creators and co-producers on their own experiences in work. How significant is this right now as a great rift opens up between employers and workers about conditions, pay and work configuration models? There has been a major transition in business. Indeed, there is a greater awareness amongst all levels of management that organizational performance is delivered through human performance. In short, stronger, healthier people create stronger, healthier businesses. This is not insignificant.

It has taken businesses a good while to realize that what happens to their workers in life will affect their performance in work. This has reset expectations on both sides. Employees have been given more flexibility, freedom and control over their lives, and it has redesigned the organization at the same time. Recognizing, supporting and encouraging humanity may seem like a natural thing to do, but it is not. Clearly – given the role of corporations in trying to claw back this new-found freedom in work and turn back the clock to when all employees were in the office the majority of the time. This is a delicate opera that is playing out in real time and as yet no clear model for work has emerged victorious. Indeed, this tension is leading to record-breaking stand-offs between workers and companies. Workers feel forced into a position where striking or protesting becomes the only option to assert their voice in this debate while securing pay that keeps up with inflation and enables them to live during a cost-of-living crisis.

TIMELY STRATEGIC ACTIONS

- Expand and scale listening/feedback practices. Enable with impactful technology where necessary to scale the co-creation of EX projects.

- Advance central data analysis capabilities to help tell a complete brand story in relation to EX. Fragmented and disconnected projects need to be brought into the fold and the strategic communication narrative to highlight the quality of the EX for current and prospective employees.

- Continually engage with peers and the organization about human performance and factor this into the EX strategy. Human/people performance is the key outcome of the EX and we need to talk less about isolated outcomes (like engagement, which is only one of many outcomes of EX). Performance and experience develop together.

Leadership

We'll go over the reinvention of leadership for the EX era in a later chapter, but it is worth noting some of the pressure on this element and what we need to think about if we are to generally strengthen this area. This is a critical issue that has emerged, alongside much needed capability development and enablement of frontline and middle-management centres around senior leadership decisions in particular. There is, as noted, a strategic and ideological ongoing debate about the best way an organization should be configured in terms of producing desirable outcomes, mainly productivity. For EX strategy, decisions of this kind may well sit above the pay grades of EX practitioners and leaders. Remote, hybrid or in-person workforces are the options before senior management in how they connect people to their businesses, and I must say there has been a creeping reversion to autocratic management archetypes on this. Employees are given a taste of freedom when it suits businesses, and it is immediately clawed back once calmer times return. I'm afraid employees are having none of it, and rightly so.

I don't necessarily take issue here with the work model that employers ultimately opt for, but I will call out the way that businesses get there. It is the ivory tower way that businesses approach their decisions – it often undoes a lot of the great work on EX and trust declines as a result. These decisions, and their subsequent implementation, are naturally at the behest of the CEO who has a particular modus operandi that they want for the organization. This is then dictated and mandated for all, irrespective of what workers actually think about the proposed – and I use the word proposed lightly here – change and how it affects them. It goes against everything EX is meant to be – co-creation, human centricity, and in no small part, empathy for people and their choices about how their work gets done. This will be the undoing of many companies.

It is also puzzling to see companies who have done the hard yards delivering positive experiences for employees then shift to an autocratic and inhumane approach to creating mass layoffs. Again, all that trust, all that respect, and all that related brand advocacy lost into the ether. Have they learnt nothing about people and the overwhelming power of their experiences? I get that in tough economic times hard choices and decisions must be made, but it's the *how* that people feel and remember, and there is still some work to do at these major moments that are directed entirely by an organization's senior leadership. There is a question sometimes that springs up at the time employees leave companies and it is related to whether or not they leave in good standing. This impacts references, both positive and negatively. The very same is becoming true for employers too. Employees have a wide range of opportunities to ensure the world knows if their former companies remain in good standing with them. It's an issue and opportunity that needs to be made repeatedly to senior leaders. It is such a shame to waste all that exceptional work on EX with poorly formed or implemented decisions made by the top team.

The onus on the EX movement has now positively shifted beyond the HR function into all support or employee-facing services and has continued to rise in prominence amongst senior, middle and junior management. This is very good and welcome progress, yet there is a big opportunity to ensure that once the top team is engaged and leading EX that they remain firmly committed to its principles in whatever circumstances present themselves for the business.

TIMELY STRATEGIC ACTIONS

- This is a work in progress, but EX practitioners are well advised to educate, inform and keep inspiring the most senior business leaders about the impact of their decisions on and beyond EX.

- Continue to build human-centred and EX capabilities across management lines. Recognize and build communities of practice to highlight and disseminate people-first management practices.

- Review leadership development, promotion and recognition infrastructure. Is it aligned to and enabling positive experiences in work?

Structural performance

If you were a structural engineer, you would look at the structural design of most organizations and conclude they are not fit for purpose, or put another way, not fit for purposeful organizations. I've noted there is still some considerable work to do in getting teams combining well to bring up top performance for EX. Yes, teams can do some journey mapping and personal development, and yes, they can perform really well together on certain aspects of redesign, but we really need a bit more ambition in this element.

Many companies that I've worked with have gone all in for EX and brought all employee-facing functions under one roof. All services that connect with and interact with employees are lined up to deliver for them. No ifs, no buts, just solid work to design and deliver experiences that break the mould and serve people in better ways. Venice would be an extremely difficult place to live without all the bridges and walkways that connect the city state. The Venetians knew connecting lands and people was of upmost importance. Building centres of excellence or expertise is a great idea if they connect with the wider whole and are not detached from the people as they often are. Again, up for consideration here is what more can be done about the structure of a company and its support services to fully embrace the employee experience getting away from the unintended consequences of unintentionally created silos.

TIMELY STRATEGIC ACTIONS

- Determine if the employee-facing structure (HR, IT, marketing, branding, estates/campus, travel, facilities, communications, etc.) is fit for purpose in relation to EX and is serving employees in a powerful, trust-building and co-creative way.

- If not, talk to your CEO and C-suite about developing something better, which places people, relationships and your brand front and centre.

Technology performance

This has been a considerable element over the course of the pandemic. HR and EX technology have exploded in growth and many new start-ups have burst onto the scene all claiming to be the employee experience platform or solution. Many are not, but they do offer specific products or tools that are helpful in solving certain challenges within the organization. Some platforms are excellent at process re-engineering, which does a massive service to the organization in eliminating unnecessary and tedious bureaucracy. Employees are always the major stakeholder that benefits from any internal service redesign or engineering, but often the last population to benefit from easy, seamless and effortless transactions or interactions within work. Companies almost always try to give this to customers upfront because if they didn't, there would be no business at all. I do think it is worth saying again that the way EX leaders tend to approach this is to be led by humans, but enabled by technology. That's the magic formula in getting technology right across the EX, and having a clear focus on the HEX and how everything integrates and connects is worth the time investment when crafting the overall EX strategy. Technology will have an impact everywhere around the EX, of course, and it is well beyond the scope of HR given the innovations taking place in workplace design and technology.

The clear-out of the old and the commissioning of the new has been happening for a while as companies find, or even try to help create, new tech solutions that better meet their needs. The performance aspect of this is often hidden within organizations though and that's what I would advise companies pay more attention to when developing their EX strategies. If a new system or platform has come into the organization, I'd want a central view on its performance and the performance of any other technology that is currently in the organization. I'd also want to know precisely what employees do with it and how it enhances their experience and the outcomes for the business. There is a tolerance for poor performance of technology in many corporations, usually because a huge investment has been made, and then there are various follow-on clauses in the contract that don't allow the form of evolution the company wants. They may have learnt through a technology implementation what works and what doesn't, but it would be far too expensive to make any customizations, and that's when they get stuck with something dated, clunky and near obsoletion even after just a short space of time. I can imagine many corporates scratching their heads after ChatGPT came into being after spending millions on clunky employee portals, intranets and other things that will quickly be useless once the potential of sophisticated AI chatbots have hit the EX in a big and better way.

This is the other point relating to technology performance. Technology advances rapidly. There will always be something better, newer and more powerful coming down the line to enable great outcomes in work, whether by communication, connection or a coherent and consistent experience with the actual technology. This is a given, so I find it is far more important to master the human element of the business first and balance technology decisions and implementations with the more important aspect of business life – human beings. In practice then, and to the dismay of the IT and digital crowd, technology falls into the background of the human and employee experience. It's there working in the background so seamlessly that we rarely give it a second thought – it just works and people can focus their attention on the important work they need to do, not get stuck talking about which platform or sign-in to use, or how slow an approval process is, or how many different apps there are within the company, or how much friction occurs between transitions and experiences. In reality, this scenario is still all too common for those who operate outside of the leading packs within their industries. The leaders tend to be more acutely aware that wise technology investment has massive upside and growth potential, and this is becoming more factored into EX technology investment.

TIMELY STRATEGIC ACTIONS

- Audit all the EX-related technology that exists within the organization. Assess strengths, weak spots and determine how integrated all the various platforms, products and services are.
- Step into the employee journey and use all of the technology that employees experience on a daily basis. Where are the disconnects? Where does the journey transition well? Where does the journey fall flat?
- Consider the information and evidence above as you build out the EX team and EX ecosystem, and related alignments and accountabilities.

Workplace performance

I would struggle to identify one element that has stood out more over the last few years than workplace. It has often been the lightning rod topic that then brings all the other elements into the business conversation. If companies move to hybrid work models, how will this change leadership practices? How will it affect the community of people within the company if they are often away from the physical workplace? How will technology fare in enabling productivity outcomes for remote or hybrid employees? How will the structure of the company, informal and formal, hold up in a new business model? How will the well-being of employees be affected by vastly different working styles? Of course, all of these are great questions, but recently they have all been focused on the workplace and ways of working. It has been a very specific global conversation and debate – there are no signs that this debate is going away anytime soon.

Disney is one of the latest companies to pull in the reins and demand that its workers return to the office for the majority of the week. A recent memo from the returning CEO, Bob Iger, reversed course on a more flexible work model for the media conglomerate and has now mandated that workers are to be in the office at least four days a week, and not the two days a week that Disney workers have grown accustomed to (Sherman and Whitten, 2023). His announcement mirrors decisions made at other companies like Apple and Netflix. This is a sharp and dramatic about-turn from the global giant, and will no doubt influence other companies, but is this commitment to in-person work the right call?

Well, this is where it gets interesting, as other technology businesses have taken an opposing view and enshrined remote and flexible working practices into their business models permanently. Companies like Airbnb, Lyft and Spotify have taken definitive positions and they are not alone, with many smaller and medium-sized businesses following suit. If this was a global election on the future of work, I'd be primed for landslide victory for hybrid work in some form given all the data points that now exist that demonstrate the clear preferences of employees to have more control, choices and options over where and how they work. It will be hard to put this particular genie back into the bottle, so what, as EX strategists, do we need to think about when forming EX strategy? That's the tricky part as our personal ideals, and even the wishes of employees, may not be a factor in this strategic decision at all. You could present all the evidence and data you like within a business case, but if the CEO wants an in-person workforce, that's what they'll get. Similarly, if they want to sell off all the real estate and go fully remote to save costs and drive up profit, then that's what's going to happen. If the hybrid happy medium solution emerges, then that's what will come into play.

What we can do in this scenario is give the best advice and intelligence we can based on the data and reference points we have to influence a decision that is helpful in aligning the expectations of the organization and its people. Though middle ground and compromise can often weaken the overall outcome in relation to major decisions or projects, we may have to acknowledge the limit of our formal influence, so what next then? That's the good thing – we can help make it work in practice and ensure the experience is enabled and delivered to a high standard. We can also prioritize initiatives within the EX that will make the experience better for people working closely with colleagues in workplace and technology design, depending on which model your company settles on. It's not our place to get caught in the middle of debate, it's to bring good things to life that enable people to be at their best regardless of where they are. The workplace is still not a building. It's the spaces and places that enable our best work (Whitter, 2022).

TIMELY STRATEGIC ACTIONS

- Whatever work model (hybrid, remote, in-person) has been mandated (or better, co-created), seek to enable it fully by reviewing overall HEX performance in relation to the work model and prioritizing strategic actions that make a valuable contribution to it. Optimized technology and leadership capabilities may well be required, for example.

- Continue to monitor employee sentiment, feedback and data, and work with employees to make the model work in practice. Get out onto the frontlines and encourage changes to the model, where necessary.

- Drive alignment through the EX strategy and paint a clear picture about how the work model/configuration connects with the brand and its people.

Community performance

With all the issues and challenges being experienced within and beyond the organization, community is not a nice-to-have feature of company life. It is an absolutely vital ingredient of success. The fruits of all that great EX work in the last few years will revolve very much around the strength of the community that has been built with intention. The powerful connections and the subsequent collaboration that have been enabled and scaled will testify to that. If your company's EX has contributed to a real sense of belonging being shared amongst the majority of employees, then this element is performing as it should be. If not, then there is much work to do and I have to say that work will not get any easier over time. With uncertainty on the rise across the global economy, we need to be more certain about the things that matter within our companies and the things that bond and unite us. It is my idealistic side that shines through here as I say this during the biggest strikes in the UK for many years. Many organizational communities are breaking down and trust in management is in decline.

As EX leaders and strategists, it is not our sole responsibility to build a community, but it is the organization's job to move from a corporate to a community. That's what good and admired companies do. They become something more than just a group of roles driving financial returns. How hollow is that? We know instinctively that human connection is a sacred part of the human experience, and we'll need to find and co-create ways to express this within the EX strategy, placing a much fuller emphasis on relationships between people, a supportive culture and leadership that cares. These are the big things that build communities alongside keeping our promises, honouring the past and respecting contributions to the greater whole. How well is your company doing on this front? What more could be done and what can you enable within the EX strategy to accelerate this sense and feeling of togetherness? Within EX organizations, this is often expressed and cultivated at different points in the employee journey – those moments beyond the control of the manager where there is direct connection with the company or the corporate centre. What kind of experiences is the HQ disseminating, and are they creating the desired connection and outcomes? From onboarding people to transitioning them into an alumni community, and everything in between, these are special touchpoints with the company.

It is, and this has certainly been proven in my work, at these moments that we learn what the organization really is and what it cares about. Values flood through these moments and milestones, and they have to be carefully managed, else the wrong message is communicated and received by employees, and it can invariably affect performance and loyalty. We are not responsible for happiness – all that talk is a bit too grand for my liking. I view the individual as being in sole control of that as a co-producer of their own experiences in life and work. Of course, organizations can make a contribution to it in many ways though, and the onus here is creating the conditions where people can step into enjoyment – they enjoy their roles, their work, their outcomes, the people they work with, the mission of the business and the social aspects of the organization. We can help with a lot of that as organizations, and why would you want to create an organization where people don't enjoy the experience? It makes no sense, but this is not measured or reflected on very often in leadership circles.

In my mind, more mature EX organizations have improved the quality of the questions they ask. In the past, it used to be more about how good an employer was and if a company was a good place to work. Those question themes are valid and relevant, but it's time to become more ambitious. How about this: Is this an enjoyable community to be part of? Are our people enjoying their experiences in work and life? There are boundaries in place for organizations at the intersection of life and work – one fades into the other yet they are both the same, and a community is being created whether it is acknowledged or not. The real question is just how strong that community is and what they are willing to do to support each other through the good times, and through the challenging times. This takes us beyond restrictive thinking of companies and corporations into something that offers a glimpse into the beauty of human life – connection and relationships. It's time to double down on building positive communities, and our EX strategies can help enable and accelerate that important work.

TIMELY STRATEGIC ACTIONS

- Reflect on your community and the strength of the connections and relationships within the organization. Map out the strongest internal communities. Draw lessons from their progress and seek to scale great community-building practices.

- Identify strategic themes, pillars and initiatives that are deliberately and consciously designed to build a sense of community and belonging. If there is not a sufficient number, go back to the co-creation drawing board and think 'community'.

- Double down on the direct connection points between the company and employees. Target moments and milestones in the employee journey to develop further and elevate. Is the Truth (purpose, mission and values) breaking through into these moments and making a strong impression/impact amongst employees?

The Truth: towards a purposeful, mission-driven and values-centred employee experience

A *purpose full* employee experience delivers a significant advantage, but the path may not always be straightforward. The corporate world is now very familiar with purpose and its impact on business performance. Installing purpose into an organization has been a key theme in business for the last decade of management thinking. Purpose has struck a nerve in corporations as an anchor on which to build their consumer and employee brand messaging. It is helpful as a way of communicating origin stories, connecting to legacies and maintaining a razor-sharp focus on why a group of people has, and continues, to throw their lot together in the form of a company.

CASE STUDY
Unilever

I took a step back down memory lane on a nostalgic visit to Port Sunlight in the UK, which is an iconic place in the history of employment. Alongside Cadbury's Bournville, it ranks as one of the most important developments and artefacts in the history of work. It is symbolic of a company deciding to do things differently, treat workers differently and to cement the importance of the human experience into the very fabric of a business. Port Sunlight was a community that provided housing, recreation and community to the workers of the Lever brothers. Its foundation stone was laid by William Hesketh Lever in 1888 to house factory workers – a vibrant community emerged with strong connections still going strong to this day. Lever, who became the 1st Baron Leverhulme in 1917, set out to build a close-knit community like days of old and was successful in creating one of the first profit-sharing business enterprises with employees – investment was poured into the development directly to benefit workers and develop a new blueprint for a socially conscious enterprise.

Fast forward to 2023 and Unilever continues to bring forth the lessons learnt from that period of its history into its business model. In recent years, the brand has a renewed focus on the very thing that defined it all those years ago – the employee experience. Not that it left that space, but Unilever has been at the vanguard of integrating purpose into its organizational culture as a priority, engaging all employees in some impressive dialogue about what purpose is, how people can find theirs and how the brand can help them live it. Unilever is a corporate giant operating in 190 countries through over 400 brand names, and with over 149,000 employees worldwide. What it does, where it focuses and how it approaches its work on company development means something and reverberates around offices the world over. They set the tone and example for many others to follow, and it is a company revered and held up constantly for its progressive take on employment, sustainability and building strong business ecosystems.

Marrying purpose with the employee experience

Championing purpose so visibly and so practically, Unilever has perhaps not been talked about in EX circles so directly in the recent past given its intense focus on purpose. Purpose and Unilever were the match. However, in recent years, that focus has expanded to EX directly and the company has caught up fast and in a quite radical way. Taking a fragmented approach to EX to task, setting out a unified vision for EX, and growing an impactful global team that is committed to EX has accelerated the company's progress. I have had the opportunity to work with Unilever's global EX team and what I have found is a considered, thoughtful and wide-ranging approach to EX – it was a comprehensive and all-encompassing mission to bring all EX functions together under one umbrella to deliver simple, consistent, special and inclusive outcomes across the employee experience.

As the journey progresses, the company continues to develop EX capabilities and has leveraged the HEX as a methodology to scale its EX impact and daily performance across the work of global teams. Tom Dewaele, who was Unilever's global head of EX when I delivered an initial advisory session for his global EX team, summed up the kind of ambition that is required to execute on EX strategy. 'We took a leap to completely change the way that we've been working. We took a leap to become experience makers... It has been a journey... and I believe it's the right journey.' (Sarin, 2021) Driving the end-to-end employee journey, balancing digital and human touch, designing workplaces based on social capital and leveraging data to make better people decisions are all viewed to be essential in getting this right.

SUMMARY

There is no doubt a lot to think about when considering EX at your organization, but what a wonderful thing that is. To have a tour around the HEX to establish where you're flying high and where you're falling short. I think we would all be better equipped and ready to deal with challenges if we did this more frequently. The HEX has proven to be a great strategic tool for managers and practitioners alike. It helps them to raise their heads above the busyness, the short term and the details of their activities to really consider the performance of the employee experience at a holistic system-wide level, and there have been many things that have been impacting all the elements of the HEX as we've discussed. It's now up to us to move with the times, but more importantly, move with the people and move with purpose.

08

Reinventing leadership in the employee experience era

The employee experience (EX) moves well beyond support functions and any form of core experience team or practitioner community. It extends to leaders directly, and in fact, leaders play one of the most valuable roles in creating a positive employee experience for their teams and the individuals within them. In this chapter then, we'll explore how to connect and align EX strategy to leaders in a meaningful way, and the required capabilities that will form part of that work.

What I won't do here is go off on a tangent about some abstract leadership concept. There are other books for that, given it is one of the most profitable areas to write about and offer services in. Why is that? Well, because leadership doesn't come easily to most people. As industry has scaled globally, so too the demand for managers and leaders. Not everyone should be in a leadership role and perhaps this is why we hear so much about the bad managers in the corporate world; there are far too many of them as companies seek to fill their management lines. EX has brought with it flatter and more open structures, agile methods and more inclusive starting positions via a more concerted effort to distribute higher quality leadership, yet leadership remains the ire (or saving grace) for most organizations. Companies are absolutely reliant and dependent on leaders, and this will be the case for some time until leadership hierarchies evolve and employees are given core ownership for their work, impact and outcomes as a natural part of organizational life. But until then, leadership alignment to the EX is critical, as is augmentation to help leaders shed some of the more bureaucratic and time-consuming administrative tasks associated with their role. A survey by Accenture summed this up nicely; it reported that managers spend a whopping 54 per cent of their time on administrative coordination and control, a paltry 7 per cent is spent on developing people and engaging with stakeholders, and just a meagre 10 per cent of time is dedicated to strategy and innovation (HBR, 2016).

Given the current economic uncertainty, the critical challenges that leaders are facing in relation to EX are compounded by everything else that is going on and being felt by people all over the world. These are magnified by media and no one can escape their effects across the workforce, yet the scale of the challenge is almost unmatched. ExecOnline, a company I partnered with recently, is tasked with developing leaders to rise to these challenges, and it is not surprising that there are significant gaps in current leadership capabilities. This is a distinctly different challenge, as the company pointed out to me in an interview. Unlike previous periods of economic uncertainty, like the 2008 financial crash, the current uncertainty comes at a time of significant talent shortage due to the ongoing great resignation and the continuing effects on businesses of the COVID-19 pandemic. 'Employees have greater leverage to make demands of their employers than they did in the past, and more than ever, leaders need to be able to address those demands, assuage those concerns, and above all, attract, retain and motivate key talent,' said Sara Pixley, Head of Strategic Insights. This all means that organizations need leaders who are highly skilled, not just in relentless strategic prioritization, but in talent engagement as well, she adds. 'However, we find only 7 per cent of leaders are highly skilled in both areas, and unless that situation improves, it means the more pressure is put on leaders, the more attraction and retention will suffer, and the employee experience along with it.'

That statement is worth a second look. Just a paltry 7 per cent of leaders are highly skilled in leading strategy and the employee experience effectively. Couple that with the evidence that suggests workers more generally are unprepared for the future of work and there is a ticking talent time bomb in our midst. Indeed, according to a study of 3,000 people conducted by Amazon and Workplace Intelligence, 70 per cent of people have reported that they don't feel prepared for the future of work, which is a staggering statistic that demonstrates the scale of the work ahead (Workplace Intelligence, 2022). If we don't understand the scale of the challenge and why organizations are delivering inadequate employee experiences and workplaces that fail to retain the best talent, then that one statistic should be ringing alarm bells around the corporate world. Yet the capability gap is just one urgent area to address. The other is equally problematic and can drain all the power that EX holds within a flash. I'm talking here about alignment (or lack thereof).

Alignment

In partnering with companies worldwide on employee experience, it becomes evident rather quickly that alignment is a world-class problem. It's one of the best and most enduring issues within businesses still to this day despite all the advances in people management practices and technology to improve systemic performance. I venture that this continues because people are involved and alignment does not come naturally to most. A world-class problem of this nature requires a world-class response to cure misalignment issues, but where are organizations going wrong specifically?

In working with ExecOnline, I found that the leadership development firm had identified four major misalignments between leaders and organizations, and they certainly coincide with my findings working on EX strategies.

1 **Leader challenges:** Organizations say their leaders are struggling the most with maintaining team well-being and culture, but leaders themselves tell us they struggle the most with motivating employees without monetary incentives and with managing workload for themselves and their teams.

2 **The productivity viewpoint:** Organizations believe innovation will improve team performance and productivity, but leaders tell us they need support in re-evaluating goals in order to improve their productivity.

3 **The commitment viewpoint:** Organizations believe leaders are increasingly disengaged and 'quiet quitting', whereas leaders say they are only protecting themselves from further burnout – we find over 70 per cent of leaders said they were at least somewhat burned out in each quarter of 2022.

4 **The paradox of priority:** Leaders want and need more learning and development, but when provided with those opportunities, they struggle to take advantage of them due to prioritization.

The cost of these misalignments is steep. A recent analysis of Bureau of Labor Statistics data by the *Washington Post* finds that productivity has plunged by the sharpest rate on record going back to 1947, as Pixley highlighted (Telford, 2022). Indeed, misalignment is killing any prospects of productivity, and the employee experience is at the very centre of this perfect storm for business success or business failure. It's never been more significant. In stable economic conditions, companies could get away with producing a pipeline of technically good professional, but very poor leaders – not now, and perhaps not ever again, given the radical changes to worker expectations in this regard. This changes how we view leaders and its connection to EX, and also how we develop and promote leaders within and beyond the organization. I've highlighted issues with leadership and the EX before. While alignment is critical, it is also hugely important to invest in growing leadership capabilities that directly affect EX performance. Often, leadership development interventions miss the mark because they lack practicality and don't fully enable leaders to meet the moments as they present themselves within their teams. Policies and procedures are part and parcel of a responsible, well-governed, and professional organization, but everyday practices matter more – the lived experience matters more. That's why this capability and alignment gap will not be sold by doing the same things that have always been done.

Emerging leadership capabilities

It's insightful at this stage to consider exactly what are the most important emerging capabilities that leaders (and organizations) are investing in, developing or starting to apply at scale.

As the tension between economic uncertainty and talent pressures continues, leaders are increasingly focusing on the skills they need to resolve that tension without additional support from their organization.

In Q3 2022, 27% of the leaders we surveyed said resilience was one of the most important skills to navigate the current business environment, up from 23% in the previous quarter. Making decisions amidst uncertainty (34%) and change management (27%) still remain critical, both increasing in importance from the previous quarter.

This makes little sense when we consider that good strategy, people development and innovation are catalysts for sustained business success, so why do companies continue to have their leaders tied up on things that waste time, energy and resources?

Technology, no doubt, is alleviating some of this and companies are seeking solid solutions within their digital EX strategies, bringing in products, platforms and services that enable leaders to more fully play their part in EX. Technology is a big part of the equation, yet it's not the thing that most impacts employees. In everything we've discovered about EX, it is clear that the leadership approach has by far the greatest impact on people. With that, it is not one thing, but all things that the leader does (or doesn't do) that is of concern to employees. There's no need to complicate leadership any more than we should. Indeed, if we stripped it back to its basic utility and form, and also consider the expectations of people, then a conclusion can be reached quite readily: we respect leaders that lead with compassion, care and enable us to feel certain that they make their decisions and choices with the best of intentions, and with people, as well as the organization, in mind at all times. In practice, and from the perspective of employees, it looks something like this:

- Strong future direction of the team (and individuals) aligned with the business strategy.
- Strong atmosphere, togetherness and energy around the team.
- Strong trust in the leader's ability to co-create plans and take positive decisions.
- Strong confidence in a leader's competence, integrity, ethics and morals.
- Strong belief and faith in a leader's willingness to do the right thing by people.
- Strong understanding and clarity on what matters most (purpose, mission and values).
- Strong commitment to growth, development, feedback and ongoing coaching.

If we spell it out like this, then we can consider a range of actions that will increase the likelihood that this type of leadership community will prevail in the organization, and the impact of poor leadership approaches would be minimal, or less likely to occur. It is not complex at all to guarantee and promise employees a high-quality leader, and it's getting to the stage that a promise of this nature must be made.

Bad bosses derail the employee experience: great bosses elevate it

It's a very simple equation, yet it is proven true time and time again. Poor-quality leaders continue to blight an organization's EX efforts, but I am by no means anti-manager. Having experienced high-quality leadership throughout my career, I know personally the positive impact it can have on careers and lives. Conversely, I have also experienced the worst of leadership too, which does have a dramatic effect on team and individual performance and well-being. Managers are often the target for blame and ridicule with some of that very often justified, but I have no doubt that the organization (and its overall leadership team) is the accountable authority on this, and must hold the primary blame (or credit) for leadership failure (or success).

What exceptional leadership looks like, and the type of leadership being emulated and held up across the economy, is fascinating. On the one hand, we understand fully the impact that human-centred leadership has on us as people. But we are also inundated with profiles of visionary leaders and those who are technically brilliant at what they do, and they deliver compelling results, but sometimes at the expense of the people they work with. There are such strong feelings about people like Elon Musk, as a timely example, given his recent and seemingly chaotic takeover of Twitter. His leadership approach has been heavily scrutinized in real time – every decision, every email and every action as he attempts to steady an unprofitable ship, which he paid $44 billion for. From my own point of view, I cannot, given my focus on EX, conceivably defend his leadership style – I can admire what he produces and the powerful pioneering results he has consistently managed to deliver, but his treatment of people leaves much to be desired, as Netflix CEO Reed Hastings highlighted when he said that Musk is 'the bravest, most creative person on the planet… his style is different, I'm trying to be like a really steady, respectable leader, you know, he doesn't care, he's just out there.' (YouTube, 2022) Yet the real secret of Musk's overall success is the strategic goals and missions he creates. 'I am 100 per cent convinced that he is trying to help the world in all of his endeavours,' said Hastings (YouTube, 2022).

I'm not saying he's all wrong, but I'm not saying he's all right either. This is the incomplete picture of leadership many of us experience – human beings have their strengths and their failings. They cannot be exceptional at everything, nor do they possess the same amount of emotional or intellectual intelligence across the board. These things are distributed differently. The question comes down to the type of leaders we want to represent our brands to the world. Strategically, this poses some opportunities for us in EX strategy, yet it also offers up some learning that we can translate into practices. What if those big macro things were people, relationships and experiences and we had our strategic EX/HR executives executing consistently against them with the same intensity as Musk? I've encountered many an organization where the negative aspects of the visionary CEO have been mitigated and limited by an outstanding human-centred leader at the top. Yet, as we look across the organization, it is clear that if you filled your company with Musk copycats, the result would be interesting to say the least. We would either get to Mars tomorrow, or crash the company in the most spectacular way possible. It's a challenging thought, but so too is the organization's penchant for enabling and promoting brilliant idiots – those with exceptional technical skills yet lacking completely in human skills. Too many of these in leadership roles make companies unstable and unsustainable given the carnage they cause internally, and we know what the vast majority of people crave in work: stability, certainty and support.

A sound and proven solution, especially if we are committed to EX, is based on a core need to commit to enabling a much larger leadership community, and that's why companies are investing heavily to grow new strategic and operational leadership capabilities, which are more aligning to the human skills that employees wish to experience with management. This is another part of the strategic equation given the size and scale of the impact that any designated leader can have on the experience of work for employees. Every interaction, every moment and every decision counts, and warrants exploration and experimentation. The default mode for anyone working on EX is to act and lead, but act in what way? In my research, I've found that getting three things right will turbo charge leadership within the organization – the triple A is about alignment, accountability and atmosphere.

TABLE 8.1 The triple A enablers of EX leadership performance

Enablers of employee experience leadership performance	What does it mean?
Alignment	Connecting leaders to EX in a strong, robust and highly visible way throughout an organization's infrastructure.
Atmosphere	Consciously curating and guiding a positive atmosphere around the team, which significantly improves experiences, relationships, resilience and results.
Accountability	Leaders are held responsible and to account for the quality of the EX. Objectives delivered to a high standard. Measuring, monitoring and recognizing strong EX performance by leaders.

Core leadership capabilities for employee experience success

Leaders are not detached from EX strategy. They are an integral part of it, so we'll need to think about how we can join the dots between the EX, the organization and the type of leadership that is exhibited (and experienced) across a company. In practice, this means that those with responsibility for the leadership development and executive development are part and parcel of the experience ecosystem, as are the leaders that shape promotion, hiring, and recognition practices and policies. Leaders must be aligned to the EX if EX is going to prove its worth. If we think about the construct of the HEX again, we can see all the elements that leaders actively shape (and will need to communicate) throughout their roles and this will be complemented (and driven) by a series of key capabilities that have been ripe for development in the new models and configurations of work. At this stage, I'd like to highlight three major capabilities and then we can explore how we can mould these capabilities and get them serving the organization in a strong and consistent way. The thread of these core leadership capabilities manifests a path of connection and communication – this type of leadership enriches the EX at every moment that matters across the employee journey. Imagine any scenario that emerges for employees – any challenge or problem – and a leader responds by default in a co-creative, connected and communicative mode. Not only does it help employees through the situation, but it also simultaneously builds trust and respect. Trust is clearly the core challenge with leadership at any level – building and maintaining trust-based relationships is essential for business growth, and the wider health and good of the company.

Leader capabilities (in relation to employee experience performance)

CO-CREATION

We've already explored co-creation as a central enabled practice in the development of the EX strategy, blueprint and overall experience masterplan. And the additional good news is that this powerful and emerging capability has started to leak across into general management, and it's something we would want to put an emphasis on within all types of leadership development, leadership enablement and leadership alignment activities. Ideally, we can arrive at a place where this very practical capability becomes the first thought of a leader when making decisions, plans, or building up a portfolio and programme of work. There is some project management

FIGURE 8.1 The 3C leader capabilities for EX

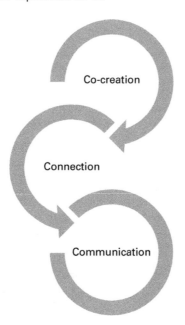

Co-creation

Connection

Communication

fatigue I've noticed up and down the economy as projects roll out as fait accomplis rather than a genuine team effort, with the active participant you would expect that goes alongside. If you've read my earlier works or taken part in some of my earlier career experiences, you'll know how seriously I apply this principle in practice. I do so, not because I'm a genius or because I'm an exceptional leader; I do it because, quite frankly, it works better than anything else I've tried or attempted within my leadership style. It goes beyond mere cooperation and collaboration, which can often be superficial and hollow.

Co-creation genuinely drives better and more enjoyable results. I say the word enjoyable because, as so often is the case within companies, collaboration on projects is not enjoyable in the slightest. It's difficult and painful for practitioners and leaders at times, and that really shouldn't be the case in a properly formed team or project. The challenge as I've discussed is that people working in their specialisms do not see themselves as part of a wider team, and why should they? Certainly, their organizations are often guilty of not setting them up in that way. Methods like agile are challenging this and bringing about some proper team experiences, yet I would like to see strong evidence of co-creation in any project regardless of the way the team or group is set up or the methodology they're using.

What does this look like in practice? That's the great thing – whatever we co-create it to be, as this capability muscle grows every time something needs to happen and involves people. I once took part in a group challenge that was assessed nationally and I was the designated leader of a group to focus on a very specific challenge. Very much in the style of *The Apprentice* where contestants have to work together but also take care to shine individually. It's a delicate balance to get that right, but the only way I know how to lead is through co-creation – I am not the commander in chief of a group of people, nor did I ever want to be. I have my responsibilities, of course, but so too do people within the team. I have my own ideas, but so too do members of the team. It's about the best ideas that deliver the most impact, and the only way to get at these is through co-creation. So, that's the way I led this group – from objectives to outcomes – and I'll always remember the feedback; the assessor sharply observed that he didn't know who the leader actually was. The co-creation style ensured we dominated the final presentations and assessment. We delivered the best ideas, the best team presentation and ultimately won the task with high praise from a leading CEO. We were poles apart from the other group, but their leader was very easy to identify. There's a time and a place for high visibility leadership, yet the real victories emerge when we focus on delivering a team experience that unlocks the creative energy and absolute best contribution from each contributor.

As I have written in my books to date, co-creation is a leadership super-power. Indeed, there is not much out there that will top this when it comes to management capabilities. It is ever present in successful EX leadership practices. Co-creation is about sharing power and bringing the full potential of people to the table. Harnessing ideas, sharing leadership and co-producing outcomes is a way of leading in a more human-centric way. Instead of dictating objectives, we co-create them instead. Instead of making plans in isolation, we create the plan together. Instead of telling people what to do, we ask them to co-create the right business-growing actions together. In this mode, leadership becomes more about facilitation and genuine collaboration than anything else. While at the same time, leaders increase and enhance all the major people metrics that matter, from engagement right through to innovation.

CONNECTION

Excellent leaders have the ability to connect people to the experiences they need at a time when they need them. Their default mode is: connect. They are constantly seeking and applying ideas that more closely connect people inside and outside of their teams, departments and functions. Leaders are the natural connection point between a company and its employees. They have the unique position to be able to connect people to what matters most to the business. Yet, at the same time, they are well positioned to connect their people with experiences, resources and opportunities that help people grow and produce their work. Leaders can operate up and down and right across the organization to leverage everything the organization has to offer to support their people. They're not exactly a concierge of EX, but they're pretty close to it when they provide access to the tools, resources and moments that employees need to get their work done to the highest possible standard.

This is also about connecting to the overall strategy of the business, its purpose, mission and values, and the overall business objectives. If people feel like they belong, it's often because leaders have connected people to experiences that count and make a difference to their everyday work life.

COMMUNICATION

EX is a collective and cross-functional endeavour. It depends on people and leaders working well together. This means that communication will need to be solid up and down the structure. Communication with employees is vital if they are to maintain a healthy connection to their companies, but what type of communication are we talking about?

Well, the style that separates the best from the rest is human-centred communication. This capability integrates things like empathy, compassion and care into a leadership style that generates positive emotions and better outcomes. It is demonstrated throughout the leadership infrastructure – 1:1s, team meetings and any situation that involves employees. The human really does come first and all else flows from there. Being human centric is a capability, a practice and even a philosophy. It has an instant and trans-formative effect on people. While communication tends to work its way up to the top of the management development list, there are some nuances in what we will be developing in this regard and what exactly leaders are communicating in the context of EX.

HEX leadership – connected, co-created and communicative

To demonstrate how we can use the HEX within the design of the team experience, we'll run through a tangible example. A make or break process within business is the onboarding experience. Those first 90 days after appointment go a long way to determine whether employees will be success-ful in their roles. It is business critical that we get this experience right as managers. We'll be thinking about and designing around all the major moments in this journey, including day one, first week, first month, first team meeting, first customer contact, first 1:1 and all the other milestones in those early stages of a new job. Let's explore some areas to consider around this experience.

TABLE 8.2 Using HEX leadership skills for onboarding

Human	We will need to ensure this is a human-centred process and is more like a *welcome experience* than a bureaucratic, management-centred process. We seek to personalize the experience where we can and use information gleaned from the recruitment process to inform its design, and to meet and exceed expectations. We give people space and support to get settled while being on hand and accessible throughout the experience.
Leadership	We're present in this process at key moments to effectively connect new colleagues to the organization, relevant networks and their team mates. We communicate key messages that role model the organization's values and give clear direction on the company's mission and purpose. Co-creating early objectives is also a key part of the leadership playbook.
Structure	We plan the key stages of the experience and design interventions that deliver a smooth and cohesive experience. We connect up to organizational resources and experiences, and design additional elements locally to successfully enable and onboard new colleagues. We guarantee a strong and supportive structure around the new employee – it becomes a platform for future success.
Technology	We can utilize technology (where impactful) to connect, co-create and communicate with new team members. Generally, we consider how and what technology is available within our teams to unleash productivity in their EX and ensure it is as seamless as possible. Companies have invested heavily in platforms and products that serve employees; managers can integrate these into their teams and encourage their usage.
Workplace	The workplace is the spaces and places that enable our best work. It is no longer just an office. Managers can design (in the context of their organization's approach) a more modern and flexible working style to suit team members and their personal circumstances. It's outcomes that matter and we can look at how the workplace serves team members in the best possible way.
Community	A sense of belonging doesn't happen by accident. It happens by design. Managers can facilitate events, social gatherings and spaces that allow people to connect at a human level. Celebrations, milestones, recognition events and many more besides create an immersive and engaging team experience. A group of people that work together and a team are two different things. We need to be more intentional about creating the latter.

Using the HEX model alongside the key management capabilities of connection, communication and co-creation that we've discussed will ensure the team experience is one that drives business growth and performance over the long term.

SUMMARY

- Explore leadership performance in relation to producing outcomes. What needs to change? Where are the gaps in capability? How can this be actively addressed within the EX strategy?

- Assess the strength of the 'triple A' leadership enablers at your organization to determine what more needs to be actioned to create the right alignment, atmosphere and accountability within and across leadership roles.

- Reflect on the 3C leader capabilities for EX and consider how to consciously develop them across all leadership levels.

- Continue to encourage leaders and managers to use the HEX as a tool, lens and resource to design and deliver positive team experiences.

09

Aligning leaders to employee experience strategy

The first thing to position on this is that there is no separation of leaders from the employee experience (EX). They are instrumental to the success of EX. EX practitioners will inevitably arrive at the conclusion that the vast majority of the most important touchpoints with employees are out of their control. Instead, they are directly under the stewardship of a company's leaders. While the EX strategy is a powerful enabler of EX and organizational performance, leaders will need to form a core part of it if the organization wishes to facilitate positive relationships from top to bottom of the organization. The EX strategy can be extremely helpful in this regard by scaffolding up the policies, practices and platforms that enable managers to play their vital roles in EX to a high standard.

Why is it that leaders have such a powerful impact on EX? In one study I was involved with across multinational corporations, we analysed decisive data that indicated what we knew to be true – leadership is an EX concern. Where leaders were equipped, capable and reliable in the eyes of their employees, the team performed much better than teams where that was not the case. Leaders with human-centric capabilities delivered high levels of trust, engagement and productivity. Much of this revolved around their own competence and capability levels – they were role models for morals and values that are important to employees. This is why leadership is viewed, rightly in my view, as a hygiene factor for a healthy organization.

The lived experience is the compelling evidence that demonstrates the quality of EX, and leaders are the primetime architects of that experience. With all the leadership infrastructure at their fingertips, leaders have the ability to enhance and enrich the EX, and this makes the leadership community the real frontline of EX, not HR or any other support function. Indeed, a redesigned team experience can make all the difference in performance terms. I've seen this so many times in practice. A change of leader signals a new era for people and performance. There have been instances where nothing about the organization infrastructure around a team has changed or improved, but a change in leader brought about major uplifts in morale, performance and engagement. This was centred on the practices, principles and behaviours they bring into play – the accountability and alignment they direct, and the commitment to help people fulfil their potential. This permeates their people-centred approach and draws on compassion, empathy and social support as the fuel for high team performance.

This is not vague or abstract leadership. It's leadership that meets the moment. It's a capability set that energizes, inspires and delivers in the present moment. Indeed, many of the top leaders have presence because they are fully present at the real moments that matter to people. They are the organization's first response to any situation or scenario. Rather than detail why this is the case, I'd like you to consider the best and worst leader you have ever encountered in your career. What was the difference between the two? Your answer will quickly demonstrate the practical human-centric leadership that is required and suited to elevate EX performance, and this is exactly the type of leadership an organization needs to promote, encourage and replicate more consistently, more intentionally across the business through whatever means necessary.

Leading the anywhere workplace

The organization is not what it used to be and the workplace has been radically altered post-pandemic. One major area of change has been the broad roll-out of 'work from anywhere' business practices. This will prove to be an important part of the EX strategy depending on what context a company is operating in. Clearly, it is a key requirement, desire and perhaps even a red line for talented workers – the ability to make grown-up choices about where work takes place. It used to be the office or the facility, now it's increasingly wherever work can be done and enabled so that people have more control over their lives; and ultimately, it is a calculated decision to unlock higher productivity and performance. Workers and organizations have a vested interest in making these policies work out in the long run, and it's an area we'll need to hone in on within the make-up of the EX strategy.

CASE STUDY

If there is one company that wants to see more nomadic and flexible work trends emerge globally, it's Airbnb, the juggernaut home rental company. Not only does it have a huge business interest in this mode of work, but it is also well-positioned to help it enable it globally. I spoke with Airbnb's people chief about this, and the momentum behind the company's 'live and work from anywhere' approach is gathering pace and is encouraging others to follow suit. The CEO, Brian Chesky, once again fronted and led this move after a strategic conversation about where the world was heading over the next 10 years, and the company built a design to fit that future – connecting people to business strategy and changing societal conditions.

Airbnb's design principles for living and working anywhere are pretty clear.

1   You can work from home or the office.
2   You can move anywhere in the country you work in and your compensation won't change.
3   You have the flexibility to travel and work around the world.
4   We'll meet up regularly for gatherings.
5   We'll continue to work in a highly coordinated way. (Airbnb, 2022)

What is positive about this is the clarity it provides to employees and workers. And it demonstrates the company is more than willing to move with the times, and of course, is astute and savvy in connecting the EX, once again, to the broader ambitions of the company to change the way the people experience the world. Following the announcement of its 'live and work anywhere' policy for employees, Airbnb reported that more than 800,000 people visited its careers page.

A connected workplace (and world)

It is tempting to restrict holistic thinking to the internal world of an organization, given there is so much there to coordinate and connect, yet the example from Airbnb shows us what EX is all about – going beyond the line of sight to actively engineer and take control of the future. Invariably, this means that those that tend to be high performing on EX are also the pioneer companies in the economy – seeking out and building trends into their business models with rapid and immediate effect. They don't wait for validation – they test which way the strategic wind is blowing and then they go all-in and set their sail for successful outcomes.

What are we doing here? We're mobilizing the equivalent populations of small cities, towns and villages to live in a completely different way and experience their and the wider world in a whole new way too. This will inevitably take the strategic dialogue beyond the borders of a company, given there are so many dependencies when considering how to enable workers in this way. Front runners like Airbnb will be keen to see national and international government policies that are friendly to organizations pursuing an anywhere workplace model as part of its business strategy, especially when it comes to global mobility.

CASE STUDY
Dell

Dell, a company I worked with recently, has embraced the anywhere workplace to full effect. This has been an evolving approach over the last decade for the company and some excellent foundations were already in place. They were more than ready to flip the switch into an anywhere workplace – where people can design their own style of working. Nonetheless, its progress has stacked up some serious wins for people, planet and performance.

- The Connected Workplace program, designed to harness the benefits of remote, hybrid and flexible work, is afforded to Dell staff and has 'saved an estimated 42 million kWh of energy. 35,000 metric tons of CO2e per year avoided from fewer commuters on the roads! Collectively, working remotely helps Dell U.S. team members avoid 136 million miles of travel per year.' (Dell Technologies, 2023) Highly significant results and a transformed work experience have taken place over time.

- The availability of the Connected Workplace program is impressive, reaching 84 countries worldwide, and is well recognized as a leading example of remote work by Forbes amongst others.

- The company enjoys broad support for its configuration of work, with 94 per cent of employees taking the view that its flexible approach to work contributes positively to overall company performance.

- The majority of the Dell workforce has accessed flexible work arrangements. (Dell Technologies, 2023)

What isn't so easy to quantify is all the joyful, and even peak experiences, that a policy and practice like this generates across a multinational workforce. From being there at special family moments, to having space and time for self-care, Dell has positively affected many, many people on multiple levels. Indeed, shouldn't a decent policy or experience design do just that? The other element to reinforce at this point is the fact that co-creation featured heavily in its design – Dell threw down the gauntlet to employees to take more control and ownership over their days by designing their ideal work configuration. It has propelled into and through a pandemic, which only served to more deeply implement and accelerate this way of working as a company. Perhaps this goes some way to explain why (out of a sample of 30,000 workers/employees) 88 per cent would recommend Dell, and to further demonstrate the connection between the CEO's leadership and EX, 96 per cent of respondents approve of the CEO, Michael Dell (see the Dell company page).

Outcomes, outcomes, outcomes

A big driving force and enabler of the last example is an organization's relentless focus on outcomes. It simply has to be that way if the model of work is configured in such a way that means people are less present in the physical workplace. There has to be a real commitment to trust and an ongoing (and open) conversation about performance, with any related tweaks or changes taking place to ensure that people and the business are (and remain) fully aligned. That's just sensible business, but business that is built and led through clear values that people see in their everyday experience of work. Given this, EX strategy will be impacted as we start to move away from an incessant focus on inputs and how people use their time. Work and time have a very odd relationship, and have formed this exclusive partnership over the years to coerce and control people in the context of Monday to Friday. I've never really understood this aspect of work. Do you pay people for the time they spend inside your company or the value they bring to it? It's a simple answer in my view, but leads to sometimes complicated practices of reporting, managing and governing time. Micro management is now frowned upon to a strong degree in management circles – leaders still do it, but it is tolerated less by businesses now and it remains deeply unpopular as an approach. Yet I can see a time where macro management could replace it through mass monitoring of employees and their keystrokes and the time they use on jobs. This is what we'll need to guard against in the EX strategy and the focus on outcomes is a good start.

The 007 principle and practice

In managing the complexity that emerges with all manner of people working in all manner of ways, businesses will need to get exceptionally good at keeping things simple, keeping things focused and keeping performance on track. Too many forms, too much stuff to remember or too many systems to navigate kills performance. People get lost in the system and leaders can sometimes be lacking in capabilities that hold everything together in a positive and supportive way. For that reason, when considering EX performance holistically, we'll need to challenge leaders to deliver clear and tangible returns.

Increasingly, data from pulses and surveys is at leaders' fingertips in some form of dashboard, but the problem is converting that data to real impact and improvement. They may get a number of areas to improve all at once and it will knock leader confidence and commitment to making a good change. Data on EX and their leadership quality can overwhelm people even if it is presented in a smooth and pretty way.

In working with global businesses, the limelight must be on a constant always-on cycle of action and experimentation. Data and insights are fantastic to have, but we also need to do as much work to deliver impact. Now, this can be done through incentives and reward, of course, and those are strong areas to explore within the EX strategy to encourage the right people-centred leadership behaviours. We need to respect, recognize and reward the things that elevate the EX. Central to this is the core need to align the entire leadership community and what they actually do in practice to lead the EX.

As a summary of the way businesses are starting to deal with this is the 007 principle and practice, which articulates what is happening in the large, complex global businesses I tend to work with. We can't expect leaders to do everything, but they can do something to affect EX performance. In this case, the summary is based on:

Three objectives & three outcomes + one giant leap (stretch objective and outcome) = improved EX performance

At an organizational level and alongside the refreshed set of leadership capabilities, the challenge must be taken up by all levels of the company to co-create and contribute to a better employee experience. The main thrust of application no doubt is fixated within the company narrative around what leaders can do to improve the EX, but as we learnt from Dell and others, it's equally about how employees can be enabled and supported to improve and take responsibility for their own EX, one which sustains business goals and performance in the long run. Timing is important here too. We know the perils of controlled time when it comes to working hours, yet having no structure around a goal is a quick way to ensure it is not achieved and no outcome is delivered. So companies are still thinking very much in terms of time when it is discussed in the context of objectives, and this very much relates to quarterly, one-year or longer-term timelines. That's the reality, though EX is challenging practitioners and leaders to think much more in strategic timelines (+3 years) for their overall programmes of work.

In-moment impact

Leadership is demonstrated through moments that mean something to people. It is an everyday practice that supports people to fulfil their potential. What has risen to the top of the leadership agenda over recent years is the core capability that is wrapped around a core need to generate and incubate more human-centric practices within the global management community. No manager has escaped the challenges and opportunities that the pandemic brought. Suddenly, managers were expected to be more human, more compassionate, more empathic alongside doing all of this in remote working style. There have been great successes and great failures as managers grapple with these emerging capabilities, but when all is said and done, it comes back down to moments – moments where human-centred leadership makes all the difference.

In-moment leadership is powerful beyond measure when it comes to meeting the expectations of employees, building strong relationships and keeping businesses right on track. Yet, to truly develop a robust approach to employee experience, there will be work to do across the organization, and especially around the day-to-day lived experience of the team.

This is where leaders become experience architects. We can define, design and deliver a team experience that gets the best out of people while creating a sense of belonging and togetherness that is a critical building block of exceptional teams. Throwing a bunch of people together, dictating objectives and running things purely in an organization-centric top-down way is rarely sustainable or healthy, and is often not very enjoyable to be part of. This is where we can make a mark and leave a legacy. To do this, we'll need to add some holistic thinking to our human-centred and experience-driven approach to leadership. The great opportunity here is to align our strategic and daily leadership actions to amplify our impact. Rising up from the moments and touchpoints with employees, we can see all the key elements that join up to meet and enable them.

Helping us navigate this is the holistic employee experience (HEX), which I presented in *Employee Experience* (Whitter, 2022). I use and continually reference the HEX with the world's leading companies to deliver strong business-growing employee experiences. It is made up of six elements that surround the most important aspects of business strategy – the purpose, mission and values of the business. I call this the Truth and it is managers who bring this Truth to life through the experiences of their teams. Indeed, leaders that successfully connect, communicate and co-create the Truth into the business deliver more profitable, productive and happier teams.

The Make a Difference (MAD) milestones for managers

Assessing the strength of the EX across an organization makes us think a lot about manager performance across the employee journey and all the milestones that matter. Each milestone has the potential to make a difference. Indeed, the MAD milestones present many opportunities to demonstrate responsible and present leadership that cuts through all the noise and resonates deeply with people. To understand these milestones, the moments contained within them, we will need to explore the relationship between the system (organization), the managers (leaders) and the people (workers, employees, partners). Management is not leadership and vice versa. There are many examples of managers who can competently manage things, yet leadership takes us several steps beyond that to create solid relationships and outcomes that exceed the normal performance levels.

Navigating key relationships and major connection points

The organization, through senior executives, sets the tone for the overall company when it comes to the purpose, mission and values of the business. The organization is also the great enabler of EX through support functions such as HR, marketing, IT, communication, estates and facilities. So, we can understand all the major touchpoints within these functions that the organization has to take care of. This covers a wide range of activities such as accessing strategic and operational information/knowledge, using communication and productivity tools, learning and development, employee benefits, internal clubs and communities, computers, travel etc., alongside navigating all the basics of employment like salary, holidays, health care and sickness policies. There's a lot to think about and design well from the organization's perspective. Leaders too have their fair share to think about and consider in how they set up and manage their teams. Indeed, much of the internal infrastructure is good to have in place to create a positive employment relationship, yet nothing is more significant than the relationship that employees have with their leader. This is underlined throughout all the activities associated with leadership, including 1:1s, team meetings, performance management meeting and reviews, and general day-to-day leadership moments. Some things and elements of organizational life will be accessed by employees from time to time or when needed, but leadership remains an ever-present within EX. It's important we get it right above all else in my view.

EX is a team game, so employees have a strong role to play in the future development, growth and success of their organization. In this sense, EX is not a done-to approach. It's experienced far more effectively as a 'working together' leadership approach. Employees are co-producers of their own experience and their role within this is not a passive one. Sitting back and complaining about the EX is not an option when employees are positioned in this way. Indeed, they are the critical stakeholder in EX.

Mobilizing positive employee experience leadership

So, we have the organization, leaders and employees all interacting across the EX every day, with lots of potential touchpoints and interactions being activated along the way. But are they positive interactions? Are we deepening our connection with people or are we letting these moments get in the way of human and business performance? To help us focus, a great first move in employee experience leadership is to identify and establish the key milestones that employees will encounter during their time with a company. These milestones, or moments that matter, are big opportunities to build a sense of belonging, create a strong impression and ultimately maintain a positive relationship that fuels performance and productivity.

EXAMPLES OF KEY MILESTONES

- Recruitment and selection events and interviews
- Onboarding experience, including appointment letters and communications, the day one experience and the first 90 days of employment

- Growth experiences, including promotions, lateral moves, mentoring assignments, learning and development experiences and recognition events
- Performance management events (1:1s, quarterly meetings, team meetings, annual reviews, town halls, etc.)
- Victories – first wins, achievements and successes
- Transitions to new roles, new teams, new challenges or new organizations (including retirement, restructures or redundancies)

As we can see, there is a lot to think about, but this really only scratches the surface. As part of their EX strategies, organizations are now looking at how to support their employees as they reach personal milestones outside of the workplace and are developing policies to deal effectively with those types of moments. Companies are choosing to assist a wide range of life events, and there is a high level of personalization in how businesses and managers help. This includes things like:

- flexible/hybrid work patterns to support people with their other responsibilities (employees are often parents or carers) or preferred work styles
- birthdays, marriages, house moves and other major events and celebrations
- leave provision including maternity, paternity, marriage, sabbaticals and career breaks
- illness, absence and personal crisis points.

The great resignation or trends like 'quiet quitting', which means people essentially down tools, check out, disengage and stop working in the interests of the organization, are very often a direct consequence of not taking the employee and human experiences seriously enough across all of these milestones that impact people. Employees will never forget how you treated them on their worst days, and they will also always remember how you supported them to deliver their best days. How we, as leaders, respond and demonstrate care, concern and empathy at these critical milestones goes a long way to determine the outcomes that people and teams produce.

We need to get them right, consistently, but what are the key capabilities that will help us to navigate the EX and all of these milestones? Given the number of potential interactions that managers have with their team members across the employee experience, they are always going to have an outsized impact on how people feel about the team, the organization and their work life in general. There are opportunities in abundance to create a connection, to co-create and to communicate with people in a way that enhances their EX.

Meeting the moment

Where can managers influence and really demonstrate their leadership capabilities to the fore? In many instances, the moments are right there in front of us, and it may require a significant shift in leadership style to affect them to a great extent. EX changes the nature of our interactions. As a way of leading, it is perhaps best summarized as a 'we, not me' style of guiding and facilitating teams. This is at the forefront of our approach and communication. We are consistently putting others first, not last. Leaders take the people experience very seriously indeed and they are proactive (and reactive) to the needs of their teams. In a sense, it's more thoughtful, considered and intentional leadership. We aim to facilitate the kind of experience that support people to achieve their best outcomes in life and work.

Here are a few practical questions that I find very helpful with this approach in leading through moments and milestones within the EX:

- Does my leadership in this moment increase trust?
- Does my leadership in this moment demonstrate that I care?
- Does my leadership in this moment show my commitment to people?
- Does my leadership bring people and the organization closer together?

These questions (and challenges) will be presented in all manners across the EX. They will require positive responses if leaders are to influence the EX and related business outcomes.

We can see how this plays out in real time. The human experience is always presenting new and unexpected challenges for people to deal with, and the impact of this leadership style is proven in moments of personal or professional crisis. In the research for my first book, *Employee Experience* (Whitter, 2022), I found that these crisis moments deliver a massive impact on people. We know they do because we are all human.

Imagine an employee approaching their manager with an unexpected and urgent personal issue. This issue is distracting them significantly and sapping their energy. It is a constant worry in their mind and it will obviously be affecting their work. Whatever this issue is, it's important to the employee and could be any one of those human milestones we've already discussed. The actual issue matters little. What matters most is our response to it, as it will radically alter the employment relationship. In this moment, we have a chance to elevate it to whole new positive levels, or erode it to the point where the relationship fractures for good. The so-called 'quiet quitting' trend could well begin to scale from moments like this, but so too is the possibility to create lifelong fans of your leadership and your organization.

The way to lead that delivers the negative outcome is to parrot company policy, focus on the work and performance issue, and to lead with zero empathy, zero compassion and zero flexibility. In short, we don't meet the moment. The employee feels unsupported, disrespected and, quite rightly in my view, will begin to question their continued commitment to your company and team.

Leading in a human-centred and experience-driven way changes all that. In-moment leadership unleashes the full influence of management on the EX. Our job in this moment is to support our employee, communicate with compassion and understanding, and to help connect them to the outcomes they need. Taking it to the next level, we will be playing the role of facilitator in that we will be co-creating solutions and ideas to overcome this challenge, using all of the resources at our disposal through the company infrastructure and also through our significant management discretion. Discretion is often understated within company policy; it is there yet often overlooked. It gives us the freedom to do the right thing in the moment and we can use this wisely throughout the EX. One colleague I interviewed said she would literally 'run through walls' for her manager based on the level of support and flexibility they received when dealing with a difficult personal issue. She came back to work having had the space and time to deal with the issue, with a renewed appreciation of her company and manager. Ten years later, and she is still talking about that moment and she remains a huge brand advocate. Meeting the moment makes a big, long-term difference.

I think of it like this: successful leaders do not win at the starting point, but at the turning point. Indeed, when I have found a successful company getting the EX right, it is largely because the managers within the company are leading strongly from moment to moment directly on the frontline of the employment relationship. What is striking though is the way they do it; they have shifted their leadership style to one that is in service to their people. Rather than commanding and controlling, they are consistently co-creating, communicating and connecting with people in human-centred ways that uphold trust, demonstrate care and maintain healthy relationships.

Certain leadership in uncertain times

Being certain about the kind of leader and organization you are becomes a strategic opportunity during times of uncertainty in the economy. Certainty in this sense means that we can firmly rely on the leaders around us, but rely on them to do what exactly? This is where the company can really inspire and shine. It's a powerful way to connect values with visible actions, and it can be an EX catalyst that inspires trust across a business. No doubt, wisdom springs from awareness and experiences; this is the next frontier in creating a more stable, enlightened and conscious management team. There will need to be deliberate and intentional cultivation of awareness across the EX – how things connect and how leaders can respond positively within those critical moments that matter to their teams. This brings about an undeniable certainty across a workforce. People want to be proud of themselves, proud of their teams and proud of their organization. Only wise and certain leadership can deliver that, and increasingly we know that certain leadership revolves around the EX.

- How *certain* are you that leaders do the right things at moments that matter to employees?

- How *certain* are you that leaders will use their discretion to create impactful experiences with their employees throughout their journey in work?

- How *certain* are you that leaders will co-create, collaborate and connect with their peers, employees and other key co-producers to deliver better work?

- How *certain* are you that leaders will put people first (in harmony with the organization's goals) throughout all of the leadership infrastructure you have?

SUMMARY AND ACTIONS

A stifling and persistent problem that I observe is that many businesses and EX teams are not certain in the ability of their leadership communities to create and maintain positive relationships across their workforces. This being the case, how can we become more **certain** that company leaders are delivering a strong EX in practice? Well, certainty is built from the ground up and the top down. The best way I have seen to do this is to focus on alignment between leaders and the business. This will naturally create more shared accountability for EX performance. This is what it will involve:

- Reimagined hiring and promotion policies and practices to drive high-quality human-centred leadership. What a company promotes creates the future of the business. Many a good business has crashed because they started to promote things that didn't advance the brand and people. A business that takes the EX seriously will always be promoting leaders who get that and apply that seriousness in practice.

- Updated capability development and immersive learning experiences that are fully focused on producing higher quality behaviours, decisions and actions within leadership performance.

- Bold (and sometimes radical) accountability practices that are designed to guarantee certainty in leadership performance. The organization will know how leaders will respond in any given moment because that's what the company will measure, encourage and demand.

- Incentivizing leadership performance around the EX, which will reward those leaders who are producing high-performing teams where people feel like they belong, and sets the foundation for strong individual and collective outcomes.

- Foundational work to strengthen the connection between functional heads and the work of their teams. I have visited HR teams that were so disconnected that no one knew what any other colleague was working on, which was remarkable given they sat in the same room. HR and support services should lead by example here and connect at all costs with their peers to drive EX performance, and role model what they expect to see everywhere else in the business.

- Curing misalignment between leaders and the organization. Leaders are employees too – there is no excuse not to be embedded within the EX approach, and any deliberate misalignment will need to be dealt with rapidly. Employees see what senior leadership do and don't do with regard to the leadership community. It's a hot topic at all times. The top team will need to be on top of their own leadership performance in the first instance to ensure the right values and behaviours are installed, and acted on, across the EX. Long gone are the days where senior leaders can take a neutral and passive position on EX and defer to HR or other functions.

10

Playing to win with employee experience

How can and how do we win with employee experience? The idea of winning is a universal one that is instilled into us from birth. There is always a winner and there is always a loser. Business is consistently framed as something we do to win. Win for investors, win over competition, win at all costs. Yet it is clear over recent years that something has changed within people and within businesses on this matter on winning. Winning at all costs is not as powerful an idea as it once was. Customers, and investors, have been historically framed as the key stakeholders and audiences in business, but no more. Employees have caught up and it is transforming organizations inside out. And it needs to be, given the seemingly endless exodus of talent across the global workforce and also given the perpetual lay-off cycle that runs alongside uncertain economic times. The world has opened back up post-COVID-19, businesses are resetting themselves and many are now questioning the wisdom that went into massive hiring cycles. Talented people have also been busy exercising their options and making new choices about where, when and how they ply their trades. The employee experience (EX), therefore, has never been more prominent than it is right now for those on both sides of the employment equation.

What does winning look like in EX strategy terms?

Winning with EX and winning in business can mean different things. There will be leaders out there that will be perfectly happy with their organization so long as the profit metric is in the right place, and the outcomes of the workforce will be of little concern. This is unsustainable yet is not uncommon.

Then there are businesses going above and beyond with EX – they do more than the basic and exceed all expectations in building great, people-centred brands.

Disney used to be a standard in the employer space. It was a company setting standards in how you build connected customer and employee experience communities, and how a one-brand story can really contribute to business performance. It is probably still getting a lot right in this regard, but Nelson Peltz, the famed activist investor, recently argued that Disney is no longer winning. It's an interesting position to take given that Disney's annual revenue grew by 22.7 per cent in 2022 to $82.7 billion (The Walt Disney Company, 2022). Citing key issues including a decline in the share price, which was down 40 per cent in 2022, Disney+ not being profitable and an increasingly unhappy (and actively protesting) workforce that has been railing against low wages in the face of spiralling inflation, there is some genuine unease about the future of the world's leading entertainment company. A Glassdoor rating of 3.9 out of 5 from employees is encouraging based on a sample size of 12,000, but pay continues to be cited as a major and persistent concern at the brand. Price gouging and constant hikes in theme park ticket prices is also painted as 'nickel and diming' a path to profit, which is viewed to be unsustainable and masking operational performance issues (BBC, 2023). Iger, the returning CEO, has already committed to a vast corporate restructure, cost cutting and lay-off drive, with 7,000 employees in the firing line and $5.5 billion in savings estimated. This is hot on the heels of other major employers cutting their workforces and reorganizing their structures, such as Alphabet, Amazon and Meta (Cain and agencies, 2023). All of this is designed to appease active investors and get profits moving in an upwards direction.

Why are we exploring the Disney example here? Because, quite frankly, it is worth pointing out the layers of complexity that the EX strategy sits in and under. Certain parts of your business may be flourishing, others emerging and others failing. Winning then is not easy to define or to grasp hold of in a narrow, linear sense. We can't also fix this incessant hire and fire cycle that the economy, and, more importantly, people suffer from. Even the most progressive and people-centred brands continue to fall into the same lay-off trap when profit takes a turn for the worse. It is an impossible nightmare for EX leaders, especially, given their commitment to building a trusted and positive community, and to see it happen time and time again can take its toll. The onus for EX leaders is to encourage responsible businesses to avoid these boom and bust approaches and all the carnage they bring, but this cycle is not going away anytime soon and it is the natural order of things currently – rise and decline.

So how do we think about this in relation to the EX strategy and our daily work? Well, as usual, it's about focusing on the quality of the experience. Even in the lay-off situation, a strong and positive brand and company can continue to move forward alongside positive and strong people who move onto different roles with other companies. A big part of EX strategy is getting these types of unpopular experiences right, and they offer a great litmus test or rite of passage for organizations claiming to be great companies and great employers.

What are the factors that indicate a winning EX and company?

In these times, there are most notably three factors that are of upmost importance in the EX. These are the non-negotiable outcomes of a positive EX in my view, and we can see how relevant they are in an uncertain world and economy.

- **Wealth:** Are employees financially stable? Are they able to meet and exceed their living needs? Are they paid fairly in relation to their industry, skills and experience?
- **Health:** Are employees physically and mentally strong? Are they in a positive place in relation to their general health? Is employee health a high priority and supported accordingly?
- **Well-being:** Are employees well on the inside? Are they in a positive state of being? Are they enjoying their work and life?

Yes, such basic questions, but how many employers contribute to negative outcomes in this regard?

The anti-hero employer scenario is not uncommon.

- Employees on low wages struggling to pay basic bills.
- Employees being pushed to deliver strong performance under the most intense and stressful conditions.
- If an employee's health declines, their wealth declines, and their well-being declines with it.

It is a domino effect and the EX will need to address all three areas in full.

It's not just about the hours people put into their work as many would have you believe. It's much more about securing that feeling that they are

FIGURE 10.1 Health, wealth and well-being

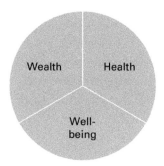

performing well (read: winning in moments, winning for people) in all areas of their life. Many a sacrifice has been made to win in specific aspects of life and it is driven by three easy-to-understand factors and motivations.

These three factors are, and will always be, significant drivers of key career decisions, and perhaps also the reason why employees choose to work at, stay or leave an employer. A deficit in any of these areas can affect the other areas instantly. We know that challenging times bring challenging decisions. The recent cost-of-living crisis is a prime example; people may well be sacrificing their health and well-being in order to secure a higher wage. There may be little choice in these decisions if people are going to pay their bills and maintain the level of life they have previously become accustomed to. Conversely, how many times do we see talented employees take lower than market salaries because they are prioritizing their health and well-being? They find and stay loyal to the employers that cultivate those things explicitly and visibly within the EX, and sometimes that is more than enough to win in the talent marketplace, certainly in more stable economic times. Yet, inflationary pressure on wages means that getting an EX geared up to serve people across these three factors is more important than ever.

John Keats, the great poet, wrote that 'nothing ever becomes real till it is experienced', and this is the case for EX. All the brand promises in the world can be made to employees, but if they are not experiences for real then they are simply not real (or true), and the vast majority of the critical impacts an employer can have on an employee revolve around their health, wealth and well-being. Keats also said that 'beauty is truth, truth beauty'. This quote often alerts me to the idea that EX is about communicating the truth to employees. What do companies really stand for? What do companies really care about? All of that will be experienced for real in the EX, so employers would be wise to prioritize continuous discovery within their work on EX strategy, as anything going counter to what they espouse will be felt strongly by their people.

CASE STUDY
Sanofi: A shared understanding of employee experience to guide global culture transformation

With an annual revenue of approaching £40 billion and close to 100,000 employees worldwide, Sanofi is one of the biggest companies in the world and a giant in the pharmaceutical sector. I've worked very closely with Sanofi in recent years to support the company's work to implement EX holistically, and it's been quite the journey to create the right kind of EX strategy that fully enables such a complex, global business to deliver excellent experiences. It's a journey made easier by a new brand that purposefully installs EX in a way that reaches deep into the organization and connects genuinely with existing approaches and infrastructure.

Ensuring EX is built up, not just bolted on

Sanofi launched its 'Play to Win' business strategy in 2019, with 'reinventing the way we work' as one of four pillars. Co-creation and co-production were at the heart of this transformation from the start, with a clear expectation that employees would play a very important part in bringing the new Sanofi culture to life. It is this, perhaps, that differentiates Sanofi.

The way the company shaped its approach to EX was to weave experiences very deliberately and intentionally into both the business and people strategies. The foundation of Sanofi's new people strategy, rolled out in 2021, was to deliver a purposeful experience for all employees. It concentrated attention on clarifying intent, and on developing concrete plans to embed purpose as part of the lived experience across Sanofi.

That compelling purpose is to 'chase the miracles of science to improve people's lives'. It is the everyday experience of this purpose that matters most. The EX is often impacted by significant factors both within and outside the organization that play a role in setting the direction of business and how that relates to people. For Sanofi, it was a series of convergent issues in the world that changed the way the business viewed and positioned EX.

'We can see how effectively and impactfully the EX can be leveraged to create meaning, connections, and tangible outcomes,' said Raj Verma, Chief Diversity, Culture and Experience Officer at Sanofi. 'The pandemic, the impact of lockdown, and intense focus on social injustice really got us to think differently and hypothesize that the game-changing trifecta for employees, new and existing, would be diversity, culture and experience. So, we created EX as a strategic enabler that connects all three drivers.'

Early strategic steps into EX

Like a lot of organizations, Sanofi took three big steps to lay the foundations for their EX strategy:

- **Commitment:** Securing support from broader leadership teams including HR (People & Culture) and developing a simple road map was the critical first step.
- **Investment:** Strategic investment in building an internal knowledge bank, creating a network of external EX professionals and leaders, and securing funding for programmes and projects cleared a path to success.
- **Communication:** Engaging a larger group of senior leaders who cover key geographies and functions was key to transitioning from ideation to operation. In a series of live webcasts, they learnt about EX as part of the Play to Win strategy and what the role of the new EX function would be across the business. I was brought in to work with this group and present my findings on the impact of EX. This engagement extended to the People & Culture function, who are key enablers of EX and need to know what's happening and why, and the role they need to play.

As Verma points out, 'It really starts with having a clear understanding of EX as an investment, not a cost in time or money, and building out a road map based on where the EX meets business needs. That starts with identifying the most obvious gaps or broken processes that affect people day to day. Prioritizing work on those gaps isn't always easy–there will always be things that need fixing – but if you don't hit the most obvious first, you don't build credibility. And you need credibility to support any business approach. What delivers that is results.'

Experience: the key strategic people theme

The Sanofi EX team engaged diverse stakeholders representing different parts of the business to help them think through the people strategy, ensuring it laddered up logically to the Play to Win strategy. They defined 'experience' as a key pillar of the people strategy, with specific focus areas built into the employee journey: hybrid working, physical workplace, well-being, recognition, onboarding, attraction and employer brand. This view on experience was supported by data from the company's new, annual internal feedback survey, called 'Your Voice'. The survey is designed to help the company prioritize global and local experience themes, and measure progress.

Demonstrating the multidisciplinary nature of EX, Sanofi's team formed close partnerships with two functions that are pivotal to change: digital user experience and research, and the facilities management and real estate. They were confident that intentional co-creation would help them deliver the right employee experience for the business.

One example was the move of Sanofi's iconic HQ in Paris, France and its establishment of a new, unified presence in Cambridge, MA, USA. In both major projects, EX and the visitor journey were anchors in the decision-making process. I was delighted to be one of the first external guests to experience La Maison Sanofi – the company's brand-new HQ on the Champs-Élysées, in early 2023. It was very interesting to compare it with the previous HQ, which was a bit colder, more detached and corporate, and not designed to bring people together.

In Paris, the collaboration created a New Way of Working change programme, with local coaches to support the transition for both managers and teams to a new workplace and new, more inclusive ways of working. Verma had a unique view on the projects as part of the steering committee, which used learning from both to establish a new workplace strategy.

'La Maison is designed to be a "home away from home", with all the modern comforts you would expect at one of the world's leading organizations. But importantly, it is the vibe or atmosphere that stands out for me: there is an openness and informality that really sets the right foundation for collaboration, social interactions and relationship-building.' That's what a modern office space needs to do, deliver positive business outcomes through positive relationships. A great office design connects people, in person and remotely, and that connection makes a tangible, measurable impact on performance, retention and recruitment.

Insights to impact

The EX team was keen to leverage external learning and bring more of the outside in, so engaged with leading experts in the market to help shape the company's workplace strategy, then build out, test and co-create with internal stakeholders along the way. This became the new-generation workplace strategy, dubbed WorkX.

Sanofi's EX team sometimes led projects directly, sometimes as co-creation partners, and often as part of a working group. Through it all, the holistic employee experience (HEX) methodology (Whitter, 2022) served as a touchstone in the design thinking process. For each project, an agile mindset helped the company arrive at minimum viable products that served as early springboards for embracing the full, end-to-end employee journey.

A multidisciplinary EX team

To achieve impact, Sanofi's EX function brought together a real mix of business and HR skills and experiences:

- **Operational HR:** A deep, lived understanding of the end-to end employee journey.

- **Strategic business partners:** Global, regional and local levels, including centres of expertise, shared services and outsourcing partners, to help create a better understanding of the big picture and what key users would typically be trying to achieve.
- **Employer brand:** Employee value proposition framework (how you feel versus what you get).
- **Marketing and brand:** Understanding insights and translating them into deliverables.

'My role as the EX leader was to connect the dots to avoid unintended consequences, which means being well networked and able to see the bigger strategic and operational picture. I also need to use every opportunity to explain and coach what is meant by EX and the methodology we use, in our case the HEX model. Otherwise, EX could be seen as just a generic common-sense activity, which has the risk of devaluing and sidelining our efforts,' said Verma.

Verma emphasized that the EX team was not about project management but a new, business-critical area of expertise, like Talent, Learning and Development, and Rewards. Clearly communicating that role to top leadership elevated the exercise of considering the EX holistically. That's how the Sanofi experience map took shape, co-created by all key EX functional stakeholders.

Planning, prioritizing and co-leadership

Sanofi's co-creating approach has been compelling from the early stages of its EX journey.

'Co-create, co-design, co-execute, co-deliver... and co-learn,' said Verma. This spirit extends beyond simple collaboration and co-operative projects. It's about taking action and getting results in a human-centred way. An obvious sign of true co-creation is the quality and robustness of the discussion between colleagues, and the actions that follow.

Co-creation in its truest form begins at the outset of any project or programme. That's why Sanofi's EX team focused on planning and prioritization as the cornerstone of its EX leadership.

'Wisdom comes from insight and understanding, and understanding the employee journey from start to finish was the lynchpin in our strategy. We gathered intelligence from all corners of the business and beyond so our decisions could be based on high-quality data. That's how we can be confident that what comes out will be targeted projects that directly impact key objectives of the business and people,' Verma explained.

This is a sign of strong, problem-solving EX work: when business and employee outcomes are aligned well. Involving key stakeholders early helped the team achieve a clear vision and align on goals, and communication was vital to maintaining early momentum. Neither could be left to chance. Including Sanofi's communication partners so they could be part of the initial thinking ensured a global perspective – one that considered everything else that was happening across the organization.

All too often, communications professionals are sought out only when things need to be announced or there is a campaign to run, but that type of approach misses the mark in the EX world. Sanofi was keen to create and maintain continuous communications, not just with key audiences, but also internal partners. To do that, an agile mindset was deployed as needed to create shared digital spaces to co-work on actions. This especially needs to be a standard practice if there is a global team in place (which for Sanofi is usually the case). Communication flows well when the basics are in place, including the project scope, alignment on desired impact and a team of people who can deliver. Winning in moments, winning for people

A solid benchmark for EX performance can be found in the moments that matter. Each moment, when optimized and performing well, can bring positive outcomes for individuals. When the company helps, supports and enables people at every moment of significance during each experience of their employee journey, they can achieve a strong impact on their brand and business performance. Sanofi is determined to create winning interactions at all these moments that matter. They are going beyond engagement surveys and pulse checks, zooming in on 'moment performance', which requires better analytics and a more focused approach to getting quick, simple, in-moment feedback at touchpoints with employees.

From the micro to the macro, EX is about major impact in the right places. In 2023 at the World Economic Forum in Davos, Sanofi launched a global initiative called A Million Conversations, which is designed to build trust in health care across marginalized communities. This eight-year project will deploy Sanofi expertise and networks to listen and facilitate real change to help create better health care experiences for underrepresented groups – a €50 million investment in projects and programmes that accelerate this also includes scholarships to encourage diverse communities into health-related careers and give them a great experience in the health care industry. Companies win when the communities around them win too.

The early work on EX has been so successful that I was recently invited to work with the broader EX team, which includes leaders from all major employee-facing functions, to document and help create Sanofi's first EX playbook. This tool is being rolled out to all global colleagues and leaders whose work significantly impacts the employee experience. This was a key milestone in the EX journey and the brand.

By disseminating HEX thinking across all EX-related projects in a way that connects to everyday work, the playbook will provide a global standard to guide each employee-facing project. It will strengthen alignment between all colleagues working on EX, and grow Sanofi's EX capabilities within the business through an aligned community of practice. Sanofi's approach to EX, from moments to major milestones, is a strong example of EX being applied and considered holistically to ensure that winning with EX is sustainable and becomes a very successful habit across all parts of the business.

Imperfect actions, but positive progress

A main difference that EX brings to the forefront within a large and complex organization is a tolerance for imperfect actions. The philosophy behind strategic leaders is less about getting things right first time, but much more about doing the right things. This involves a high-level iterative approach, but even before that, it demands a basic commitment to trying new things and seeing what happens. This naturally creates a more fluid strategy, yet it is also a more certain one. People can be certain that the organization is not inflexible about things that do not work in practice and they will be focused on creating solutions that work better. Seeing organizations that are keenly and firmly committed to EX performance rather than attempting to force experiences on workers that not only don't meet their expectations, but may also not be truly aligned to what will really help deliver those core business needs, is a very refreshing approach indeed.

The learning experience is something that ties in very closely to the EX strategy too. Listening, feedback and action cycles will continually influence the direction of strategic initiatives once they hit the real world. The old way perhaps was to carry on regardless and drive through strategic projects until they were fully operational despite negative feedback from employees or even spiralling costs, especially in relation to technology projects, but if progress is not being made then EX leaders will have serious questions to ask about their overall approach and how they design and commission things. This is where some significant learning takes place – at a strategic level. We'll be in constant learning mode about EX performance at all times, but we'll also need to consider our individual performance more closely as EX leaders. I've observed a mixed picture in this regard.

EX leaders can be tempted to make safe decisions that are not necessarily the right ones for the business. They may not be prepared to take a risk when investing in innovative EX products or services, or programmes where the value is not immediately clear. While I understand this, I have also observed many instances where EX leaders and strategists took intelligent risks to elevate the EX at their organization, and they ended up with real success stories on their hands, or signature experiences that transcended their businesses. These can be small or big ideas and investments, but what we need to do is create space for us to consider radically different ideas that go against the norm and that are aligned to the brand Truth of the organization. It is in these places that brands can differentiate their EX from others and move away from the vanilla, plain and bland EX, which is going to be an important and ongoing strategic concern.

The strategic atmosphere around employee experience

What does winning look like? Well, that's a matter for each brand to consider for themselves, but it will look distinctive and unique. It will be memorable in its own way and the personality of the EX at any given company will be different. In saying that, we don't live in a vacuum, and there will be things working really well at other companies that we may be inspired by and will make a lot of sense to learn from and apply. Yet, how we do this matters a lot, especially in communication terms. Each and every improvement or design must be fit for the context of the community, and it really ought to build on the company story and employer brand. The EX is the major part of the employer brand. It is the substance of what is promised to employees and prospective employees. It guides perceptions, but also has major impacts on overall brand performance. Building a holistic EX story allows companies the freedom to showcase and highlight the real employer brand as it is, not how companies market it to be. These two are often not the same, and this leads to unmet expectations and simmering resentment. What was promised was not delivered. This is not winning, and this is not even playing to win. In a similar vein, this chapter is not called 'Playing to be average' for very good reasons. No one really wants to be associated with average or just good enough.

People want to associate with companies that are doing exciting things, making positive impact in the world, and actually go above and beyond for their workers and employees. That is far from average. Indeed, those activating the EX are in their own leagues and are consistently held to be well above the average in their respective sectors.

In more practical terms, this is why EX teams and projects become bastions of energy and excitement. Finally, the EX is given the attention it deserves and it is always active and engaging work to get involved with. This ambience and atmosphere around EX will not happen by accident, and this is where the EX leader and team will come into their own by directly shaping it into being. This, in part, is what winning with EX means.

Employee experience is in the memory business

Every leader, professional and employee has access to their own memory, which has documented their organizational and career lives. People are the residual outcomes of their experiences in life, and memories will always be there in the background creating perceptions and reality. The organization also has its own collective memory card and it is built on what the organization does, what it designs, and how people feel and think about those things. EX then is most definitely in the memory business. It's a fact often overlooked in EX strategy, but it is a fact nonetheless.

In my career, I have often referred to institutional memory in my work. Organizations are made up of people, and people have long memories. These memories come into play and create a rich tapestry of an organization's progress and plight, and employees access this memory often when considering their thoughts and feelings about a company and their organizational behaviours. They consider how the company is designed, the decisions senior leaders take, and all the data that unlocks a real picture of performance across all parts of the business. So as strategic leaders we will need to be mindful of these memory drivers at all times and how they interact and integrate with each other, if our strategies are going to be shaping the right narrative and prioritizing the right actions.

SUMMARY

We will know when we are winning when the collective and individual memories of an organization combine to create positive feelings and outcomes in daily life over the long term. I often ask people about when they had very positive experiences with an employer – some will often have to search deeply into their memories to access a great, tangible example and to find an employer from their career history worth talking about.

Others are very different. They do not even flinch or think for a second. The brand and employer immediately springs to mind and is already on the tip of the tongue. There is no de-focusing in the eyes and no evidence of any search whatsoever going on in their minds. They know the employer they want to highlight immediately and they do not hold back in their praise, respect and admiration for what their example employer did and how they did it. In almost all cases, the universal feeling is of connection, belonging and support. They felt their employers cared about them, trusted them and treated them like human beings. In my view, that's what winning in EX looks and feels like.

11

People experience: bringing beauty to the world

A positive employee experience is, quite frankly, a beautiful thing. It's something of beauty – to be admired, to be studied and to be showcased throughout the world. Everything works well and flows from one moment to the next across the holistic employee journey, and the people and business outcomes are rich and uncontested. There is often a coinciding and non-negotiable belief at senior executive level that business outcomes are entirely dependent on people so, at the very least, people should have a positive experience in work. Now, this is far from universal and I do tend to work with the top-end employee experience (EX) companies around the world that have earned the respect of their people and others besides by investing in EX early and heavily. For our EX strategies to create a thing of beauty then, we'll need to explore the ugly side of employee experience in this chapter first.

Some of the things I hear about EX within developing EX organizations are now well-established themes within people professions. I stress the word 'developing' from the previous sentence. Many leading EX organizations have already been through and started to answer these challenges directly. Largely, because as they have evolved their EX approach, they have encountered expected and unexpected problems and issues that have halted, but not derailed, progress with EX. I share some of these challenges here for reference and we can have a look at them in more detail. They will, no doubt, be evident in some quarters as we build and launch EX strategies.

Insights from the frontline of EX

There has been some incredible progress with EX, and the gap between intention and execution is getting smaller all the time. A recent poll I conducted amongst hundreds of large employers found as much, and now a majority have formal EX strategies in place. The challenges then are designed to prompt even more accelerated progress with EX and to deepen the related EX practices into the business. While this is not an exhaustive list, these are some of the key talking points that come up when teams begin to navigate their way into an EX approach at their organizations. These are, perhaps, the things that are unhelpful in positioning something that looks, feels and sounds like a beautiful experience in work.

1 Consultation is a crutch, genuine co-creation is lagging.

Sincere co-creation, as we've discussed at length earlier, remains something that will be in scope for a much-improved focus when developing and contemplating EX strategy. It is not exceptional EX work if we are merely sitting in ivory HQ towers dreaming up plans to take to employees as a fait accompli. Co-creation is not about giving employees options that the organization favours – that's called rigging the experience game and it won't deliver anywhere near the best outcomes a more co-creative approach would. Consultation is a management approach of last resort. It is easier to just take pre-prepared plans and ideas to the workforce, but then struggle to get buy-in over the medium to long term. That turns into hard work based on a failing 'them and us' approach to business. Better to enable employees to create solutions to their own issues and problems with exceptional support in place from the EX team and managers to do just that. Businesses grow through the ideas, inventions and innovation that comes from the people themselves. Embrace that, don't hide from it within EX strategy.

2 HR is still focused too much on HR.

Another ugly truth about applying EX into practice is that HR is still predominantly focused on traditional HR things. That can be stifling for EX as newly minted EX managers are expected to work within the HR organization and on HR-owned polices, processes or elements of the employee journey. This is, of course, good work to do and there will be any number of employee journey projects to work on, improve and develop. For sustained and powerful impact though, EX leaders really need to be positioned beyond HR and their roles should reflect a business-wide interest in EX and in daily work experiences. If we can help people do their jobs better in the moment with customers, clients and consumers, then that is where the really powerful and valuable EX can be done. Not unusually, EX teams tend to focus their early efforts on the HR realm, yet the more advanced or wise EX leaders will always be seeking gains across the holistic EX, whether through authority, influence or inspiration. EX feels right when it is a genuine business and brand leadership role, and is not indefinitely anchored to any one function. Doing it in that way avoids EX becoming viewed as simply one function's responsibility. The truth is that EX is a business responsibility.

I'll again reinforce the need for deep change within HR, but I've spent a good proportion of previous books on that and my position hasn't changed at all. HR needs to evolve with the times – the rise and new prominence of people and experience functions is an indicator that this shared point is breaking through, as is the influx and rapid growth of all EX roles up and down and across company structures. I said it would take a while for HR to transform and that is turning out to be the case, but some major brands have already moved to people functions, and that trend is gathering some serious momentum. If the substance changes with them and companies continue to develop EX capabilities across their teams, then those from HR backgrounds can look forward to a very bright people-centred future.

3 Managers are not strongly aligned to EX.

We've already spoken in depth about aligning managers to EX and it is one of those things that makes all EX work less beautiful. There may be a great EX team in place and all support services are playing their roles in EX, yet if managers remain detached from EX work then momentum will stall and dry up eventually. It is critical that EX is disseminated and enabled across the organizational structure and that managers are accountable for the quality of their contributions to their team experiences. Capability building has already begun in earnest across organizations and the economy, but it still feels a little too abstract and removed from the everyday experience of work. EX leaders will need to drive leadership outcomes via any means necessary, including leadership development initiatives and all the related management infrastructure including hiring, firing, promotion and recognition practices. A beautiful EX demands high-quality human-centred and experience-driven leadership. It's time to give employees what they want and need in this regard, and more consistently too.

4 Alignment between functions and practitioners needs to be stronger from the outset of EX projects.

It sometimes takes a while for organizations to bring functional heads together to work on EX. This is puzzling for several reasons. Perhaps EX leaders and the organization are still finding their feet and don't want to appear vulnerable when discussing a new management approach or sharing knowledge that they are not fully confident about themselves, but it would be wise to get the ultimate co-creation team together at the earliest opportunity. When this happens, what you look at and explore from an EX improvement perspective, changes, and it can change quite rapidly, as can the ambition the organization has for EX. It can uplift everything. Yes, do the research, get yourself briefed on EX and perhaps some early thinking about where to improve and what to work on, but don't hold fast to those things until a cross-functional EX ecosystem has been stood up on. On behalf of the organization. Why wait? There will be some projects that get the EX work moving, but there is no good reason to not start working on EX holistically from day one of the EX strategy. Co-creation is a big part of the strategy and it needs to be role-modelled throughout.

5 Technology is never the answer to solve the holistic EX challenge.

It can be quite an ugly thing to see practitioners jump the gun and reach for a technology solution in the very early stages of the EX strategy. I do think EX leaders are guilty of moving a little too fast on the technology front at times. Yes, they have things to deliver at scale and technology will certainly have some of the answers on that, yet it is not wise to rush into commissioning major technology investments in EX prior to doing some of the really valuable groundwork. Indeed, technology can sometimes exacerbate some of the issues that are being faced with the EX and also some of the misalignment between functions. It is not a beautiful EX if all we do is flood the EX with technology that employees don't want or need, and worse, don't even use.

Technology, when considered as part of the holistic EX, is incredibly powerful and can be very helpful in scaling EX outcomes. Still, too much technology that used to be something else is being branded EX and repackaged for enthusiastic EX audiences, and not enough due diligence is going on about the true impact that some technologies really have on actual EX performance. This can be easily solved though. Technology is part of the answer, but only one part of the EX. Technology alone is not what EX is really all about.

6 An emergent Truth and trust gap is under greater scrutiny by employees.

What companies said they were and what they valued prior to the pandemic has been under ever greater scrutiny as employees experience knee-jerk reactions, authoritarian diktats about how their workplace experiences are going to be, and a total lack of trust from management layers that have been, at times, completely out of their comfort zone giving up control and power as employees work out of sight in their own homes. Employees, rightly in my view, have become deeply sceptical about the intentions of their companies because actions have not been meeting grandiose words and value statements in practice. A positive employee experience builds and maintains trust. It is, in my view, one of the most powerful outcomes of EX when applied well. Trust goes up and stays up, which creates great relationships and related business outcomes that emerge out of those relationships. It's a simple formula for EX success – build trust through the touchpoints and by connecting people to the purpose, mission and the authentic (real) values of the business. A lack of trust in an organization makes for an ugly business. Leveraging the EX to form deep levels of trust within an organization creates great beauty on the inside as well as the outside. Employee experience and trust don't often get tied together, but they should be and this means that we are more conscious of our actions, decisions and behaviours at all times to ensure we're having a trust-building impact across the EX.

7 Treating people as human beings is still not the business default. Will it ever be?

Linked to the last point, another ugly truth about business is that we are still only at the very beginning of our human-centred journey. It may feel like two steps forward and three steps back sometimes, as companies react to various pressures and personalities in their decision-making philosophy. Without a deeply ingrained respect for people within the business model, these challenges will not go away fast and it will be very confusing for people. In surveys at companies that are not clear on where they stand with people, I observed a total lack of clarity about a company's intentions and how highly they think of employees. Let's be clear, employees should be in no doubt whatsoever that a company has their back through the good and the bad times. The EX is an excellent way to communicate that point through everyday human-centred practices.

8 Short-termism and inconsistency can scupper EX efforts.

Adaptable organizations will always outlast those that are stuck in their ways. Indeed, a trait I've noticed at companies that have managed to operate across eras and over longer periods of times is that they will adapt. It's in-built into the very fabric of the organization. They adapt, but they are not reactionary. What remains solid is an abundance of care when dealing with business headwinds and the impact they have on people. Even when repositioning and lay-offs are required, there is a display of empathy, care and respect for people.

Many companies have been found out in this regard through and after the pandemic. They may have been excellent at leveraging their EX to attract top talent, but decisions since have left them faltering with worker revolts, protests and huge disconnects between what the company says it is, and what it actually is. A people-centred approach to business and a long-term view on the value of people must be woven into every facet of the company, and it really needs to be as consistent as possible. The feeling that an employer cares and respects its workforce transcends physical geographies. It can be adapted, contextualized and translated in many ways for different and diverse audiences, but that feeling can remain strong wherever it occurs. That's an aim of a positive EX – to go beyond the short term and think much, much more about creating human-centred business that lasts over the long term.

Thankfully there are many companies out there that are challenging old paradigms and setting new expectations about the world of work.

CASE STUDY
L'Oréal

L'Oréal is a company that rarely needs any introductions. Valued at $11.2 billion and with over 86,000 employees, it is the most valuable cosmetics brand in the world, and has also earned its reputation as one of the world's top employers. Having worked directly with the company and its EX team for over a year, I have observed first-hand how this 100+ year-old company has forged ahead with EX, and crafted and co-created a people experience strategy that has generated real momentum across the business.

Visionary experiences

L'Oréal has wasted little time in setting its vision for EX. The people vision at the brand is to *be the most inclusive, innovative and inspiring people-driven company to create the beauty that moves the world*. As visions go, this is as bold as it is ambitious, and it is reflected in how quickly the brand has progressed its work on EX to date. There is an urgency and excitement about the work on the EX and as the movement grows and more people become aware of the work, the vision acts as a compelling and unifying force that helps connect people, teams and objectives.

L'Oréal's founder, Eugène Schueller, was the company's revered first people leader. He once said that 'a company is not walls and machines, it's people, people, people'. It is this statement that cuts through the most about how world-class and world-leading brands are created. This people philosophy transcends everything, and I have seen first-hand at L'Oréal how this focus on people is incessant and never-ending. It is a part of the brand's DNA and it is integral to its success. In this sense, formalizing this into the company's first people experience strategy and team was a natural step to take.

Relentless focus on people, rethinking what's possible with employee experience

During those early stages of the EX work, I observed at close quarters the passion and enthusiasm for improving the lives of people that is now synonymous with the EX field. In L'Oréal's case, the people experience has become a vehicle to enable beauty and beautiful experiences to flow through the organization, and the EX is being led globally and across regional markets to do just that. Beauty, of course, is often in the eye of the beholder, and the company has also looked to personalize experiences as much as possible to connect with people individually throughout their employee journey and their daily work. Why can't we have beautiful experiences in work every day? *Why can't we create the most people-centric company on the planet?* This burning desire to rethink what's possible for EX was incredibly inspiring to witness, and the company is asking the right questions and challenging people to think differently about the experience of work.

'The People Experience approach is about dedication to what is the most precious to us: our People. It's about obsessively wanting to augment the experience at every moment; from the daily ones to the ones that matter the most. It is a powerful way to re-inject further people-centricity into our organization,' said Claude Rumpler.

Harnessing potential, prioritizing actions

Starting with several bigger EX projects, the mobility experience was an initial target for improvement on a cross-functional basis. A team of colleagues from across functions were brought together to define, design and prototype a refreshed approach to mobility. With coaching and facilitation sessions, the team worked through their ideas, conducted research and presented a range of options that were designed to enhance the overall journey. Not only did the project deliver some solid prototype outcomes, but it was also a test case for how the company can develop successful multidisciplinary and cross-functional teams to work on EX at a global and regional level.

What was interesting about this approach is that it immediately set EX as a business approach rather than locking it up and concentrating on any one function like HR, for example, which is often the main instigator or custodian of EX efforts. To be more holistically successful, EX will have to be applied, designed and considered at the holistic level. The employee journey and all those associated moments live beyond and between functions, so this often changes the way companies build agile teams around the EX. These teams can then operate quickly with flexibility, and can mobilize actions effectively in dotted lines that connect colleagues and teams on the structure chart.

A co-creation community – bridging experiences

L'Oréal has developed an approach that enables its leadership team to strategize alongside a community that triggers actions. Aided by augmented listening practices and augmented journeys in work, the brand is on the front foot of change and transformation across the holistic EX, with well-being and acculturation of people set as a high priority across the employee journey. These are deemed to be the outcomes that will turn the people experience into a major competitive advantage.

Co-creation really starts with the first follower. The colleague who is brought in at a global level to orchestrate and guide the people experience agenda for the organization. In this case, Claude Rumpler, Head of People Experience, was the person charged with initiating the people experience movement that has a long reach into all parts of L'Oréal. From the outset, I worked closely with Rumpler as he set out to create the people experience strategy for the brand. I can tell you that co-creation started from day one as he navigated the organization's structure chart to map existing EX performance, roles and capabilities.

The term 'experience bridges' was something I coined during a strategic workshop at L'Oréal because that's exactly what the company was doing with its co-creation efforts. People with influence and accountability from across the EX were brought together in Paris to ideate, share and develop the people experience priorities and strategic themes. As I reflected on the wonderful dialogue and thoughtful reflection, I could see in real time that bridges were being built between functions and people in the spirit of harmony and a shared interest in the developing powerful people-centred experiences at the brand. This is fine EX work and a phenomenal way to enhance the impact of our work on EX from the get-go. Developing strong cross-functional and cross-cultural bridges is a strategic EX priority, as Rumpler highlights.

> We have been gradually building a core cross-functional squad including internal communication, digital experience, real estate, facility management and listening; stretching towards additional functions like learning, IT or data depending on the moment focused on.
>
> It is fascinating to see that the more the teams worked together, the more we discovered and valued our interdependencies. The People Experience approach

conducted us to go beyond departments, silos and egos to focus on what matters most: 'our People'.

Beyond moments that matter – people experience dashboard

From the outset, the brand has looked to improve a wide range of moments across the employee journey, but it has also prioritized and categorized elements that enhance daily work. How can we make a positive impact in daily work and the everyday experience? This is a thoughtful question and takes us far beyond moments and milestones along the employee journey. This is an important distinction to make, as EX efforts can often be concentrated on the bigger projects rather than the projects or targets that can make an immediate and long-lasting difference for people as they go about their business every day. This is where EX can cut through the noise and make the greatest impact and impression on people.

To achieve the people experience vision, data was required, and lots of it. The brand was careful to accelerate this at the start of its work on people experience, and that has proven a wise move with key projects now coming to fruition, including global and local pulse surveys to leverage the voice of the employee at all points in the journey. This all builds into key performance indicators for the people experience strategy that can be used for monitoring and enablement across the organization. A big part of this work is to also inject the brand Truth into each and every moment across the employee journey – infuse the organization's DNA (purpose, mission and values) into the EX.

The key here though is to be in a state of continuous learning that helps the company to improve and elevate people-centred practices, while eliminating any pain points that are identified in the employee journey. As an EX team, the feeling was that they wanted to care even more about the details – because it's in the details where great beauty can be found and experienced by employees.

Workplaces that move people

Being immersed in the L'Oréal experience is about experiencing beauty on a daily, moment-by-moment basis. It is no surprise then that the brand already boasts a world-class estate and continues to evolve this still further with state-of the-art workplace experiences a major part of the overall EX at the brand.

The EX is a physical and virtual manifestation of how healthy and strong a company really is. To this end, the brand is consistently focused on improving daily work outcomes and how people experience and relate to their workplaces. Another key aspect of this immersive workplace experience is to honour the past, the heritage and the history of the brand. In many ways, we build from the past into the present, and that connection will determine our future. The rich history of the brand is never far away from practitioners' minds and this naturally flows through the work of the EX team into tangible projects that immerse people into the brand experience.

One L'Oréal

Only a holistic approach to EX can be effective in delivering a purpose-infused journey in work. Purpose has traditionally been at the forefront of the brand's consumer business, and instilling its purpose into the EX is a high priority. The path to purpose is found in the EX – what people are immersed in every day – and this is what makes a beautiful and well-crafted EX. Purpose alongside other augmented journeys such as digital ways of working, the on-site experience and moments that matter naturally leads to a more coherent, connected and stronger EX. Balancing the individual with the brand has also been an important part of this work, and that's why a more personalized experience is a foundation stone in the overall strategy.

At L'Oréal, there are six values that people are immersed in every day. They act as guidelines for people and leaders in their daily work, and help maintain a pioneering spirit throughout the workforce. They are:

- passion
- innovation
- entrepreneurial spirit
- open-mindedness
- quest for excellence
- responsibility.

The people experience is now positioned as a primary communication channel to embody, role-model, exemplify and enable these values across the employee journey.

'The People Experience approach goes beyond enabling an always-on flow of innovations to augment experiences. It also turns into a virtuous spiral as each Moment on the journey has a unique potential to instil purpose. Ultimately, it is a powerful enabler for our People to blossom within our Why, in a world craving for more humanness,' said Rumpler.

Under passionate, committed and skilled strategic leadership, L'Oréal has already made giant strides in its work on EX. It is maintaining a rapid pace across a wide-ranging portfolio of EX projects, and real community has formed around the people experience. The company has been quick to create an EX team and ecosystem, building experience bridges between functions, and is growing a high quality set of EX capabilities around the world. A beautiful EX moves people, businesses and the world to deliver better outcomes – L'Oréal is at the very forefront in making that a reality.

Going deeper into the people and human experience

Naturally, as the EX approach grows and matures, attention will turn to the people and human experience – businesses will more clearly understand how the employee and human experiences connect and how that drives performance gains and outcomes. This is evident because a large number of companies have workforces now made up of many different constituents. Gig workers, contractors and contingent workers have very definitely come into the mix when considering the scope of the EX strategy. For many though, the main thrust of the work on experiences will remain in the employee space and they will then broaden out things that work into other populations. There is no tension or conflict here. It is simply the evolution of business, and I have discussed this at length in my previous book, *Human Experience at Work* (Whitter, 2021). Not all experiences have to be the same. Not all experiences have to be standardized. There are business choices in this regard, particularly when developing the EX strategy. Yet, the main area for discussion is how a business treats people. Whether employee, supplier, contractor, customer or shareholder, our work on EX should further a connecting and sense of belonging amongst all supporters of a brand.

The holistic EX, certainly in my teachings and advisory work, transforms into the human experience very quickly. The deeper we go into EX, the more humanity we will see and actively design our organizations around. This is very healthy progress in strategic terms. For me, the strategic focus is where it should be – experiences and the quality of them. This is the right direction and companies can also exploit and maximize all the in-roads that have been made through customer experience practices. Indeed, there will be a lot to learn from customer experience (CX) strategies, what has worked and what hasn't in how we approach strategies for employees. Yet, as I've high-lighted before, EX is not merely CX on the inside. Employees are not primarily customers – they enjoy a deeper and more connected relationship to the business, and that needs to be respected at all points.

Beautiful designs, beautiful outcomes

There is still this tendency within HR and other support services to think of internal work on EX as merely functional and organizational improvement when it goes well beyond that. The experiences that are designed or redesigned can touch people's emotions, increase their well-being and make the world a less confusing, more certain place. It is a gift and privilege to do this kind of work and to observe the very real and genuine impact that it has on people. Bringing those feelings of joy, belonging and trust into the organization is not easy work to do, yet EX leaders and practitioners have the capabilities now to affect things quickly by virtue of their actions. What does this mean in practice? Well, we need to starting thinking about the total end-to-end experience of the employee journey and all of its constituent parts. Beyond getting the functional mechanics and processes right, we can add some beauty to things we co-create through more intentional aesthetic design, more thoughtful connection to the company brand and more alignment with the people within our organizations. For this, EX strategies will need a heavy dose of marketing and communication expertise as part of the co-creation team. The communication, PR and marketing teams are those that can enhance the reputation and credibility of our EX work. Not only that, with our efforts we can light a path for others to follow while attracting the right people to grow the organization in the right way.

At times, sometimes there is a world-class experience occurring but no one knows about it, and even employees simply take it for granted and rarely give it a second thought. This matters in strategic terms because if people don't realize how good they really have it at your business, they may well end up moving to your competitor to find that out for themselves. With boomerang employees becoming more and more common, there is a renewed line of thinking within EX about making sure our communication practices are always on. The story is always developing and being told, and it's a narrative driven by the people within the organization. Employer branding and employee value proposition (EVP) often sit outside of the EX strategy, and I'm not sure if that is the right call given the discussion here and within the field. What would be helpful is bringing EX and how it is communicated together as closely as possible. There should be no gaps between the brand, the people and their experiences, and it is this story arc that will generate interest, excitement and passion about your company and the opportunity to work for it.

Beautiful experiences, beautiful people

Every person is beautiful in their own way. There is something that stands out about them, and there is something that defines and differentiates them from others. The EX is one of the most sustainable ways of celebrating that beauty and that difference on a daily basis. Through experiences, we can view our own potential and that of our organizations. In this sense, beauty is attainable within every company – we will just need to develop the EX with wisdom, in the style that suits our people and business, and in a way that builds a long-lasting connection with all stakeholders. As practitioners and leaders, this means the people experience at work takes on a whole new level of reverence. And why not? This is not a simple body of work. Working with humans is complex and can often get emotional, and to do this with skill, compassion and empathy is where EX strategists come into their own. By raising standards in how we think about organizational work, we can start to see even bigger opportunities to affect EX performance and raise ambitions in relation to the mandate and the movement we have. For EX practitioners are artists, sculptors, architects, painters and musicians; they help bring an organization to life and create the kind of beauty that is evident every day and in every way across an organization. It's the kind of beauty that's not just skin deep.

12

Conclusion

No one has ever promised that working on employee experience (EX) was easy. Indeed, it is the challenge of a career to truly lead and help to install EX into the organization as the default and dominant approach in achieving people outcomes. Yet, it gets so much easier if leaders co-create and co-lead the EX strategy across the business. If we can share our power with people and leaders, we can accelerate our progress with EX on all fronts. That's what an inspired strategic approach gives us – it puts the EX work on the front foot and sets the tone for what follows it, and what follows is usually strong and targeted actions that make a difference for people and the brand. While great care needs to be taken in aligning the EX strategy to both people and the organization, not simply one or the other, the benefits of doing so are numerous.

Answering strategic questions about ourselves

In digesting all the information and guidance within these pages, I'm sure you'll be looking forward to getting stuck in and start designing the EX strategy for your company. But before you do, let's perhaps take a step back and consider what this strategic approach gives us directly as leaders and professionals. Leading and developing strategy at an organization-wide level is not something to take for granted. It is a huge privilege and with our actions we can have immeasurable positive impact on those we serve and those we are in service to. There are some things though, as a pragmatist, I'd like to draw out for your attention.

When starting to co-create and work with the organization on strategy it can be tempting to be a source of answers – to be the expert and the knowledge in the room. Many fall into this trap and assert their dominance and authority over a particular domain of organizational life. They set out to prove something or another, and demonstrate their expertise at all points. EX leaders are somewhat different in this regard and it's worth highlighting what that difference actually is.

For me, I've spent an incalculable amount of time developing the EX field through coaching and advising the most senior EX leaders within a company, coaching their teams, and generally working with colleagues and clients that are ready for EX. What I've noticed time and time again is that by far the most effective and impactful EX leaders are the ones who don't have all the answers and don't claim to be experts on the topic. They defer to employees, partners and others, and set out to leverage the expertise of their co-creation partners. It is never about them, it is always about the brand, the people and the organization.

Brand leadership through EX

Strategic EX leadership sets colleagues apart because they do certain things in a certain way. That's perhaps an apt sentence to describe what they do best. They bring certainty to people that the organization cares, can be trusted and is working to help people become the best that they can be – in life and work. Never claiming or wanting to be viewed as some kind of perfect authority, they present in a way that is disarming, inclusive but also inspired by the possibilities that EX brings forward. They are the archetype brand leader – caring for people and the organization that enables them. There is no conflict in this regard: for people to be strong, the organization must be strong too. Of course, several more things stand out about their approach to building EX strategically, not least their commitment to co-creation, connection and communication to get things done, but also their willingness to try things, experiment and fail as necessary. Though their kind of failure is always about failing forward, learning from setbacks and challenging the organization to be better than it was yesterday. That approach is not failure of any kind in my view.

As they move forward with EX strategy, they also light a path and signpost the way for others into EX. It becomes a shared moment, a shared movement, and authority goes into the background – in this sense, EX leaders can be the great organizational unifier, and part of their approach naturally establishes several important aspects within their own personal experience.

Credibility

EX leaders develop credibility with their peers, senior leaders and employees by role-modelling EX practices within their own work, teams and functions. They do what they ask of others, leading from the front initially as a catalyst, but they are equally happy to fade into the background to give people the ownership and autonomy they need to take full responsibility for EX outcomes. Giving power away is harder than it sounds in practice, but they are keen to do so to deliver outcomes and sustain team performance. EX leaders literally co-create their way to credibility.

Clarity

EX leaders, due in no small part to their obsessive focus on people and their experiences, create clarity in their organizations. Clarity about what EX means to the company and its people, but also clarity on how everything fits together and the related performance of all those parts. They paint a complete picture for maximum organizational gain. Yet, at the same time, they ensure clarity is maintained and developed for employees at all levels too, but this clarity is more concerned about demonstrating that the organization cares, is committed and trusts its employees, and can be trusted as an employer. This is what strong EX work yields in abundance – a new or renewed perception and appreciation of the organization and what it stands for.

Coherence

Part of strategic EX leadership is to help the organization make sense of itself. To hold up a mirror and sincerely ask if this is what the company wants to be. The truth is found in the EX and they are very keen to share it with others to prompt change. Leading beyond their function is normal and natural as they seek to scale up a coherent EX that is aligned to what matters most within the organization. A coherent and holistic employee experience that makes sense on paper and also levels up organizational storytelling is something that only wise leadership can deliver.

Challenging and co-creating with the status quo

We have to be effective with what we have in strategic terms. Whatever circumstances or issues present themselves, that's what we'll be working with. There's zero point in complaining about something that will not change. This is where EX leaders excel along the employee journey, finding ways and means to make those minor and major gains in partnership with others. Lack of budget or lack of support rarely gets in the way as showstoppers in their EX efforts – there is always something to be done and there are always willing co-creators within a business – we just have to find them and bring them into the EX fold. This is also what good EX strategy delivers – positive and productive cross-functional relationships where real value is created. The status quo in your company – it is what it is, but that doesn't mean that's what it will always be. We'll need to put a lot of effort behind our communication practices to extend the impact and involvement in our work on strategy, but let's not forget that the process of designing a strategy is an excellent and wise way to build healthy networks, teams and well wishes in support of EX performance. The whole thing about bringing a strategy into being is that it's an excellent way to engage with people, learning about their priorities, and perhaps how they can get aligned and contributing to the EX strategy from the get-go.

Employee experience is a question of time

Whenever the concept of time comes up within the organizational context, it tends to be centred around employees. How can they effectively manage their time in work and manage it appropriately to be more productive and less stressed? The idea of time management though shouldn't be the exclusive domain for personal accountability. When EX is applied effectively, it is usually associated in some way to time. This makes perfect sense, doesn't it given that people trade their valuable time for a salary? That has been the basic level exchange between employers and employees – time.

Yet, a more enlightened view is starting to take hold in business and this basic time/money transaction is being challenged within the EX strategies of today. EX leaders are more consciously focused on value rather than time, and that is rewiring companies from top to bottom. The headline-stealing initiative in this regard is the four-day week. The excitement around this is palpable and it is now being positioned as a big part of the future of work. What are we saying here with developments like this? Well, employers are saying very clearly that time is important throughout life and work, and they are striking a better balance based on the expectations of workers and employees. Companies are giving people time back to spend in ways that raise the quality of their human experience while receiving more intense and focused periods of work time where things are still getting done, and, usually, much more besides.

Shopify, the e-commerce giant, has joined companies like Citigroup, Twilio, Meta and Atlassian in purging what they deem to be useless and time-draining meetings from the business. There are now meeting-free days mandated at the business, alongside other meeting controls that are enforced by a bot about the types of meetings people can attend and take part in. This takes place at a time when the company has been downsizing its workforce by 10 per cent (Nawrat, 2023). It is experimentation with time as the company continues to learn from its foray into becoming a work from anywhere organization during the pandemic. Yet, looking across the EX we can see how much of our impact is based on giving people:

- fast internal technology-enabled transactions and touchpoints throughout the employee journey
- timely career design, development and progression support
- time to provide feedback, praise and share learning about their EX
- high-quality time with their families, friends and loved ones
- the ability to urgently respond to any personal crisis with full support
- the space and time to focus on their well-being, health and wealth needs
- time with their manager to discuss their EX and experience real-time coaching and mentoring
- the opportunity to define and make choices to personalize their EX and way of working in a way that enables their lifestyle and personal circumstances
- policies that are human-centred and ensure quality time is built in to experience the milestones of life/work (maternity, paternity, house moves, birthdays off, etc.).

The list is endless! It is that way because time is the most valuable resource human beings have. Employers that respect and revere time will naturally consider any practice, policy or experience that takes time away from people unnecessarily. This perhaps offers some explanation as to why heavily archaic and bureaucratic organizations are loathed by employees – they are time stealers, literally, so it's no wonder employers are stepping into to force changes through in this regard, and if those interventions are co-designed with the person in mind and are established to unleash their potential then even better. The real headline here is that the EX strategy is a great foundation on which to make the most of time across the organization; this will benefit the brand, human and employee experience in more ways than we can imagine.

Every X matters

As the EX field matures, so too does its connection with the other Xs. The customer, brand, shareholder, community, supplier and worker experiences all connect and amplify each other. The same holds true for X leaders too. The more each respective leader embraces the experience that they are focused on, the more they realize they are dependent on others. To become a world-class brand and company, there is an inevitable conclusion that experiences all around the brand must be of a very high quality.

Several global clients I work with understand this fully. They are amongst the most ethical companies in the world and have the awards and certifications to prove it. To become a supplier to a brand like that, my company was assessed on its ethical standards based on how we do business and interact with the world. Many companies protect their brands and experiences by ensuring the high standard they set is internally also met by vendors, suppliers and partners. The connection matters and it is increasingly the case that companies will formally take a stand and defend their principles. EX is a huge part of this and our wider EX strategy will need to ensure that the connections between all stakeholders around a brand are progressing the company in the right direction.

Strategic milestones, moments and momentum

EX performance, as we've discussed, is built from moment to moment. EX management platforms and dashboards can be very helpful in making sure performance stays on track and the strategy is doing what it was co-created to do – affect people and organizational performance positively. The sense that real progress is being made across the EX will not be hard to establish if we consistently keep an eye on the performance of each and every touchpoint with employees across their journey in work. There will be a wide variety of owners for moments and milestones along the journey and EX leaders will need to get really good at sharing and discussing performance in relation to EX. The great thing about EX is that performance cannot be hidden in plain sight – the experiences, from pre-hire to retire – are evidenced daily and will be significant markers of perpetual progress. Have we simplified processes? Is it easy and efficient to find the information we need? Do we have the right tools to do our jobs? Does this experience bond me more closely to the organization and the people within it? Does this moment immerse people into the Truth of the business? Does each experience enhance and elevate our well-being? Is the employee journey strong, coherent and connected – does it feel like a compelling story is unfolding? Every strategic intervention and improvement will create a story, an impact, and a ripple within the company. In performance terms, we need to ensure that it is a positive story that is being told and experienced daily by employees, as this is where strategic momentum will come from – positive outcomes and the related anecdotes, statistics and research that brings that to the surface of the collective consciousness around the company.

Humanizing HR (and all support services) continues

Predictions about the impending decline of the HR profession have proven true at a global level and with challenger companies that have been questioning the merits of the traditional organization and how it builds communities. These companies don't steal time from people, they tend to steal fans and market share from their less progressive competitors. Which would you pick? A company focused on EX and a positive employee journey, or a company that continues to treat employees like kids and payroll numbers? No heavy maths is required to deduce which companies employees prefer, and preferences count, especially when talented people are costly and hard to acquire. The early pace-setting multinational corporations have seriously shifted the entire profession (and all the roles and teams within it) well and truly into the people space.

Getting the HR house 'in order' is often a first step with EX to sort out messy processes or painful experiences that are dealt from HR services, tools or products, and while it's a good step, a far more effective approach for EX, as we've discussed through these pages, is to share responsibility for it quite quickly. If it starts life as HR-owned and stays there, that is far from ideal. The EX strategy has the scope to challenge this narrative and positioning, especially if a strong mandate from the C-suite is also in place. Yet, in saying this, HR is a vast and well-installed profession, and humans as resources is still there in the corporate lexicon. Time will change this unless there is a collective management lurch back to control, authority and power over people that they once enjoyed en-masse around the world. I'm inclined to be optimistic about this, given the newer generations are demanding fast and rapid changes to the organization as we know it – to be more social, more ethical, more planet and people friendly. These are positive trends and companies will have to continue to move with the times.

A lot of talk about humanizing HR relates to the policies and procedures of the function. There is so much potential for a painful experience to be manifested directly out of HR policy. Indeed, the policy and performance suite associated with HR can be problematic in building healthy relationships, and some often run counter to that objective. Disciplinary, grievance, capability, absence management and others tend to leave a lasting impression. At the very least, these policies need to be humane, but ideally we should be looking at all these policies to assess what the organization (and its community) needs to do about them. What do I mean? Well, for those who have spent a decent amount of time in the EX field who then go back and reflect on the HR policies and practices of the day, it can be a challenge not to want to make considerable revisions immediately. Human centricity and our focus on experiences changes the way we see things and the outcomes we can potentially create. In any case, HR continues to have a strong role in EX and we should use that role wisely to move closer to the business and people – and this includes the HR business partner model in its entirety. There can be a lack of alignment with that valuable group of colleagues sometimes within companies who are bringing in EX as an approach. As a strategic approach, HR business partners will need to start seeing EX as a core part of their role and how they lead their work. For this, capability development is going to be a key development to drive the behaviours and practices that fully unlock the potential of EX from project to project.

However, things have already changed in a considerable way. Historically, if the EX went wrong, it would be HR that faced heavy criticism. Not so now. EX naturally expands and shares accountabilities for performance outcomes, both positive and negative, so it is becoming an increasing challenge for heads and directors of other functions that interact with employees to avoid serious scrutiny. The other positive aspect of EX is CEO culpability. The correlation between EX and CEO leadership is now written in stone thanks to employee ratings platforms like Glassdoor. Positive EX, positive

CEO is a nice pattern across great brands and organizations, and the CEO role in EX is significant to say the least.

I worked with a senior HR leader recently. Before finding one of my virtual certification programmes, EX was not even on their radar. They'd never considered this idea of experience and how it can be co-created and co-led holistically. They mentioned that the programme has radically transformed the way they look at the organization and its people. There is no moving away from EX as a management concept – it sticks, it's effective and it brings about lasting positive change. There may be reactions, power grabs and lurches back to a more organization-centred model, but our job is to keep the organization and managers centred and sensitive to the quality of the EX on a consistent, sustainable basis.

Present moment performance

The present moment is all we have. Right here, right now is what always matters. The past and the future live in the mind. A good EX strategy yields higher quality present moments in work and life. It is a defining yardstick of overall EX performance.

- Does the employee journey deliver when employees need it most?
- Is daily work enabled effectively so people can prioritize things that grow themselves and the organization?
- Are any disruptions or problems with performance in the present evaluated and dealt with swiftly by a unified EX ecosystem?

Any delays or inaction on EX will inevitably contribute to weaker overall performance. Likewise, any delays in capability building programmes that develop leaders and practitioners that make the most of the present moment will affect performance. As part of our monitoring efforts, it will be a wise move to ensure that all of the colleagues that interact with employees have what they need to make excellent choices, excellent decisions and run excellent projects. A sign that an EX ecosystem is in a healthy state is the speed at which improvements can be made across the company.

We can test this in real time now. If a pulse survey, or other body of data and insight, surfaced a pattern of feedback relating to the same painful experience along the employee journey, how long would it take your organization to mobilize and fix it? The only acceptable response is fast or very fast. I treat employee issues the same as I treated customer issues when I worked in the customer experience (CX) field early in my career. Nothing should get in the way of a positive experience. The extent to which your organization is set up to be agile will affect this greatly, yet there are many ways to mobilize and scale rapid actions within the business. Indeed, if the organization looks like a spider's web, our role is to facilitate and maintain that web as much as possible in a quick fashion, or the whole web – its strength and longevity – will be affected negatively. Once again it comes back to what we can do in the present moment and in real time. This means that our capabilities, connections and the communities around will need to be consistently robust under challenges and pressures.

The AI-enabled employee experience is here

For many organizations, using chatbots and AI capabilities across the EX will still be feeling like something beyond their scope and something that is really rather alien to them. Chatbot market growth is expected to hit $3.62 billion by 2030 (Straits Research, 2022) and Gartner has forecasted that 50 per cent of knowledge workers are expected to be using an AI-driven and chatbot-based executive virtual assistant by 2025 (Bradley, 2020). There has certainly been an uptick in chatbots serving the EX during and since the pandemic as EX services are augmented by AI and chatbots to run conversational processes and transactions across the employee journey. The groundbreaking launch of ChatGPT by OpenAI and subsequent integration with a popular search engine has created massive interest (and trepidation) about what is coming down the line from technology generally, and its applications in the workplace. The announcement of such powerful chatbots that upend industries and create such a strong reaction from the general public is testament to their potential for good and for bad. It's going to be fascinating to see how this evolves and we need to start exploring this topic right now to benefit our work on EX while remaining ultra-focused on balancing humans and technology as part of our holistic employee experience (HEX) thinking. I've said it before, and I'll reinforce it again here: without checks and balances in the system, the connection between humans and technology may get weaker before it gets stronger. We need to tread very carefully here in how we strategically augment and automate elements across the EX.

AI's benefits for humans could be 'so unbelievably good that it's hard for me to even imagine,' said OpenAI CEO Sam Altman (Roose, 2023). Given these emerging capabilities, I am optimistic that EX-minded leaders will be the difference here and help translate new technologies into the work context while maintaining that laser-like human-centred focus. If they don't, there will be many more strategic people challenges on the way, especially in larger organizations that release chatbots, AI and augmented practices in an iterative state. The backlash against ChatGPT and the criticisms it has faced regarding the accuracy and sometimes nonsensical nature of its output since launch is a good example of why calm heads and considered steps will be required with such advanced capabilities like this being unleashed within organizations.

Driving strategic EX progress

EX is now the primary driving force behind the organization's work to install the purpose, mission and values of the company into everyday work and the employee journey. The companies that excel at this will create greater outcomes for all the stakeholders around a company. The organizations that fail to act now will miss the boat and will likely get swept away from the sectors and industries under a disastrous (and entirely preventable) wave of anti-employer sentiment. The record-breaking wave of strikes that are going on around the world offers a glimpse of what more is to come unless employers get their EX strategies right in the first place. The leading organizations on the planet tend to place their bets early and heavily, and the bets they made on EX several years ago have been keeping them at the top of their markets and in the public eye for the right reasons.

EX improves everything and the learning experience evolves with it too. Indeed, the more an organization learns about EX, the more they learn about the reality of their organization and how it affects performance. This insight changes what people learn, the defined capabilities that people need, and it also transforms how people apply the learning in practice. Learning is applied in a tangible way to elevate people and the organization at the same time. In this sense, driving strategic EX programmes will depend a lot on the quality of the learning that takes place within EX roles, teams and leadership generally, and how fast that learning is action to affect EX performance. How quickly can your team turn insights into actions? This is a good measure of EX maturity and how strongly you can progress EX within your context.

We've only just begun

We have come to the end of our strategic exploration of employee experience, yet our journey continues indefinitely. There is always another problem to solve, another experience to improve and elevate, or another advancement in our understanding of what matters most within EX. This is the natural order of things, and we should cherish this work that has the potential to affect so many people – employees, families, shareholders, partners, community, society and the planet overall. In my view, the very best businesses are co-created with people. They are built and maintained together. Every action, decision and experience has the opportunity to strengthen (or weaken) the organization and its people, so it is more important than ever before that we enable people in the best possible way.

There is now a worldwide community of leaders and professionals that are moving the EX forward every day through their example, and through their compelling strategic leadership. They, together with employees, are literally reshaping what we know to be true about an organization. Indeed, the very idea of the organization has been challenged, and EX leaders have been at the forefront of radical changes and experiments that redesign work and redesign lives. The employee and human experience are more connected and more important than they have ever been within the corporate world. Our EX strategies and their impact will make that connection ever closer to the great benefit of our companies.

As I mentioned earlier in this book, enjoyment is not a metric that is often talked about within EX, but maybe it should be. Employees enjoying their experiences in life and work, and organizations enjoying strong growth, performance and productivity. These things can all be achieved in harmony and I encourage you, as an EX leader, to help make it so through your work on the EX strategy. Enjoy the experience.

REFERENCES

Chapter 1

LinkedIn (2023) 'LinkedIn Jobs on the rise 2023: The 25 UK roles that are growing in demand': www.linkedin.com/pulse/linkedin-jobs-rise-2023-25-uk-roles-growing-demand-linkedin-news-uk/?trackingId=iq4Fs7YZQteBIOY07J29HA%3D%3D (archived at https://perma.cc/NTK3-Q6BR)

Chapter 2

American Psychological Association (2022) Inflation, war push stress to alarming levels at two-year COVID-19 anniversary: www.apa.org/news/press/releases/2022/03/inflation-war-stress (archived at https://perma.cc/R9XZ-SEYS)

Bove, T (2022) 'Prepare for a "long and ugly" recession, says Dr. Doom, the economist who predicted the 2008 crash', Fortune, 21 September: fortune.com/2022/09/21/long-ugly-recession-dr-doom-nouriel-roubini/ (archived at https://perma.cc/MZR2-UREE)

Chung, F (2022) 'Fears Credit Suisse is on the brink of collapse', News.com.au, 3 October: www.news.com.au/finance/business/banking/fears-credit-suisse-is-on-the-brink-of-collapse/news-story/38b7f2d35116cc565820e93a1ce8a6d9 (archived at https://perma.cc/28DN-AG6H)

Hipkiss, R (1986) Jack Kerouac, Prophet of the New Romanticism, University Press of Kansas, page 83.

Ito, A (2022) 'Inflation is 8.3%. Raises next year will average 4%. Do the math', Business Insider: www.businessinsider.com/salary-increase-2023-projections-raise-inflation-jobs-wages-income-2022-10?r=US&IR=T (archived at https://perma.cc/VHS2-2PTF)

KPMG (2022) 'KPMG 2022 CEO Outlook – UK: Growth strategies in turbulent times': assets.kpmg.com/content/dam/kpmg/uk/pdf/2022/10/kpmg-uk-ceo-outlook.pdf (archived at https://perma.cc/K8BM-S3H2)

Microsoft (2022) 'Hybrid work is just work. Are we doing it wrong?' Work Trend Index Special Report, September 22: www.microsoft.com/en-us/worklab/work-trend-index/hybrid-work-is-just-work (archived at https://perma.cc/NMU7-D242)

Whitter, B (2022) *Employee Experience: Develop a happy, productive and supported workforce for exceptional individual and business performance* (2nd edition), Kogan Page, London

Chapter 3

Hogan, K (2022) LinkedIn post, September: www.linkedin.com/posts/kathleenthogan_dont-let-cynicism-undermine-your-workplace-activity-6972920802023288833-r1Yq (archived at https://perma.cc/LK48-MB4J)

Whitter, B (2021) *Human Experience at Work: Drive performance with a people-focused approach to employees*, Kogan Page, London

Chapter 4

Amazon (2023) Leadership Principles: www.aboutamazon.com/about-us/leadership-principles (archived at https://perma.cc/2BBP-L25V)

Whitter, B (2022) *Employee Experience: Develop a happy, productive and supported workforce for exceptional individual and business performance* (2nd edition), Kogan Page, London

Chapter 5

ExpressVPN (2022) Survey reveals surveillance fears over the metaverse workplace: www.expressvpn.com/blog/survey-reveals-surveillance-fears-over-the-metaverse-workplace/ (archived at https://perma.cc/Q4PP-63DT)

Hackl, C (2021) Defining The Metaverse Today, Forbes, 2 May: www.forbes.com/sites/cathyhackl/2021/05/02/defining-the-metaverse-today/ (archived at https://perma.cc/JU3H-UH2V)

The Guardian (2013) 'Grand Theft Auto 5 – inside the creative process with Dan Houser', 13 September: www.theguardian.com/technology/gamesblog/2013/sep/13/grand-theft-auto-5-dan-houser#:~:text=It's%20up%20to%20us%20to,seeing%20the%20limitations%20in%20games%E2%80%A6 (archived at https://perma.cc/PDY9-NXPS)

Chapter 7

Sarin, B (2021) Tom Dewaele on Unilever's digital EX journey, September: anz.peoplemattersglobal.com/article/employee-engagement/tom-dewaele-on-unilevers-digital-ex-journey-30799 (archived at https://perma.cc/X394-8KGX)

Sherman, A and Whitten, S (2023) 'Bob Iger tells Disney employees they must return to the office four days a week', January: www.cnbc.com/2023/01/09/disney-ceo-bob-iger-tells-employees-to-return-to-the-office-four-days-a-week.html (archived at https://perma.cc/3CMV-XY96)

Whitter, B (2022) *Employee Experience: Develop a happy, productive and supported workforce for exceptional individual and business performance* (2nd edition), Kogan Page, London

Chapter 8

HBR (2016) 'How artificial intelligence will redefine management', Harvard Business Review: hbr.org/2016/11/how-artificial-intelligence-will-redefine-management (archived at https://perma.cc/5MJ8-LNVP)

Telford, T (2022) 'U.S. workers have gotten way less productive. No one is sure why', The Washington Post, 31 October: www.washingtonpost.com/business/2022/10/31/productivity-down-employers-worried-recession/ (archived at https://perma.cc/F7FU-7UJH)

Workplace Intelligence (2022) Study finds that 74% of Millennial and Gen Z employees are likely to quit within the next year due to a lack of skills development opportunities, 27 October: workplaceintelligence.com/upskilling-study/ (archived at https://perma.cc/5F56-DJWM)

YouTube (2022) 'Where does Netflix go from here?' with CEO Reed Hastings, The New York Times: www.bing.com/videos/search?q=Reed+Hastings+Elon+Musk+&view=detail&mid=84FCAB381AEC9CBBA3F884FCAB381AEC9CBBA3F8&FORM=VIRE (archived at https://perma.cc/3FG8-Z7M9)

Chapter 9

Airbnb (2022) 'Airbnb's design for employees to live and work anywhere', 28 April: news.airbnb.com/airbnbs-design-to-live-and-work-anywhere/ (archived at https://perma.cc/T9CY-2GC5)

Dell Technologies (2023) 'Work Life Balance – See how our team members around the world find balance in their everyday life': jobs.dell.com/work-life-balance#tab-panel-1-1 (archived at https://perma.cc/829P-EQU7)

Whitter, B (2022) *Employee Experience: Develop a happy, productive and supported workforce for exceptional individual and business performance* (2nd edition), Kogan Page, London

Chapter 10

BBC (2023) 'Disney accused of squeezing theme park customers', BBC News Business, 12 January: www.bbc.co.uk/news/business-64255871 (archived at https://perma.cc/3XVU-RFPR)

Cain S and agencies (2023) 'Disney announces 7,000 layoffs while teasing Toy Story and Frozen sequels', *The Guardian*, 8 February: www.theguardian.com/us-news/2023/feb/08/disney-job-cuts-savings (archived at https://perma.cc/89SR-D3TP)

The Walt Disney Company (2022) 'The Walt Disney Company Reports Fourth Quarter and Full Year Earnings for Fiscal 2022', 8 November: thewaltdisneycompany.com/the-walt-disney-company-reports-fourth-quarter-and-full-year-earnings-for-fiscal-2022/ (archived at https://perma.cc/PF4B-ZRZ4)

Whitter, B (2022) *Employee Experience: Develop a happy, productive and supported workforce for exceptional individual and business performance* (2nd edition), Kogan Page, London

Chapter 11

Whitter, B (2021) *Human Experience at Work: Drive performance with a people-focused approach to employees*, Kogan Page, London

Chapter 12

Bradley A (2020) 'Brace yourself for an explosion of virtual assistants', Gartner, 10 August, blogs.gartner.com/anthony_bradley/2020/08/10/brace-yourself-for-an-explosion-of-virtual-assistants/ (archived at https://perma.cc/A4US-JQS5)

Nawrat A (2023) 'Shopify encourages employees to say no to meetings', Unleash News, HR Technology, 5 January: www.unleash.ai/hr-technology/shopify-encourages-employees-to-say-no-to-meetings/ (archived at https://perma.cc/2USV-MZUV)

Roose K (2023) 'Kevin Roose's conversation with Bing's chatbot: full transcript', 16 February: www.nytimes.com/2023/02/16/technology/bing-chatbot-transcript.html (archived at https://perma.cc/TS54-FR4W)

Straits Research (2022) 'Chatbot market growth is projected to reach USD
3.62 billion by 2030, growing at a CAGR of 23.9%', GlobeNewswire, 29 June:
www. globenewswire.com/news-release/2022/06/29/2471371/0/en/Chatbot-
Market-Growth-is-projected-to-reach-USD-3-62-Billion-by-2030-growing-at-a-
CAGR-of-23-9-Straits-Research. (archived at https://perma.cc/6M4E-5LDS)

INDEX

Note: Page numbers in *italics* refer to figures and tables

8XP framework 53–60, *58*

Accenture 107–08
activism 29
  campus activism 11
  employee activism 23
AI (artificial intelligence)
  capabilities 172–73
  chatbots 98
Airbnb 100, 123, 124
Algorithmic HR 3
Alphabet 136
Altman, Sam 172
Amazon 55–56, 108, 136
American Psychological
  Association 20
Apple 100
Atlassian 167
augmented reality (AR) 70–71

Bournville 104
brand 2–3, 12, 13, 17, 56, 94, 96,
  101, 134, 171
  brand leadership 164–65
  brand leadership role 151
  employee brand 104
  employee experience, understanding of
    (case study) 139–44
  EX understanding 52–53
  EX vision 66–67
  experience mindset 67–68
  holistic approach 45–48, *47–48*
  L'Oréal (case study) 154–59
  people and human experience 159–61
  people-centred brands 136
  performance tracking 168–69
  rusted and positive community 135–37
  team performance 77–79
  see also employee experience
    performance, planning
Bureau of Labor Statistics data 109

Cadbury 104
Cambridge 141
capability gap 108

capability(ies) 5, 27, 31, 95, 108, 110, 114,
  117, 121–22, 127, 134, 170, 171
  AI capabilities 172–73
  EX capabilities 105, 144, 151, 159
  experience mindset 67–68
  leadership capabilities 108, 110–11, 113,
    114–19, *115, 118*
  performance 59–60
  strategic challenges 44
careers 9, 10, 52, 56, 71, 79, 122, 143,
  146, 163
  career decisions 138
  career journey 2, 73–74
  cross-functional career mobility 6
challenges 11, 13, 56, 75, 86–87, 149, 150,
  166, 169, 170, 172, 173, 174
  co-creation 114–16, *115*
  critical challenges 108
  employee experience, universal
    approach 42–43
  EX vision 66–67
  experience mindset 67–68
  human-centred challenge 3–4
  in-moment impact 127–28
  leader challenges 109
  management idea 1–3
  organizational challenges 82–83
  performance 59–60, 92
  strategic challenges 44
  technology 152
  see also co-creation; employees
Champs-Élysées 141
change management 39–40, 110
ChatGPT 98, 172–73
Chesky, Brian 123
chief people officer (CPO) 3, 9
Citigroup 167
co-creation 12, 27–30, *29*, 114–16,
  115, 152
  campaign 39–40
  challenging and 30–31, 165–66
  consultation 150
  EX, strategic approach 163–64
  L'Oréal (case study) 154–59
  people and human experience 159–61

co-creation (*continued*)
    performance tracking 168–69
    requirements 31–37
    transformation 37–39
    universal approach 42–43
    see also employee experience, ecosystem;
        EX teams; experience masterplan;
        HEX performance; workplace
colleagues 73, 74, 76, 155–56, 170, 171
    brand leadership 164–65
    co-creation community 156–57
    8XP framework 53–60, *58*
    employee experience, holistic
        approach 45–48, *47–48*
    employee experience, understanding of
        (case study) 139–44
    employee experience, universal
        approach 42–43
    employee journey 4–7
    EX understanding 52–53
    EX vision 66–67
    experience mindset 67–68
    financial crisis 20–21
    global pandemic 9–11
    mindset 7
    organization, map of 69–70
    people leaders, emergence 2–3
    people strategy 16–19
    return on experience (RoE) 92–93
    workplace performance 99–101
    see also co-creation; EX teams
communication 8, 9, 39, 44, 53, 70, 98–99,
        114, 117, 119, 131, 140, 143, 145,
        160, 164, 166
    high employee experience
        performance 81–88
    L'Oréal (case study) 154–59
    relationships and connection
        points 128–29
community 2, 6, 64, 78, 93, 104, 134, 136,
        144, 158, 168, 174
    co-creation community 156–57
    community performance 101–03
    global management community 127
    leadership community 55, 111, 113,
        121, 126
    practitioner community 107
consistency 37, 46, 84, 86, 153–54
consumer brand 66
COVID-19 pandemic 19, 108, 135
creativity 39
Credit Suisse 19
customer experience (CX) 3, 33, 49, 53, 63,
        68, 159, 172

customers 33, 56, 64, 68, 98, 135, 150, 159
cynicism 37

data 2, 8, 57–59, *58*, 60, 78, 93–94, 100,
        121, 146, 157
    employee experience, understanding of
        (case study) 139–44
    EX understanding 52–53
    laws 82–87
    LUCK 32–37
    work and time 125–28
Davos 143
decisions 57–59, *58*
Dell 124–25, 126
Dell, Michael 125
design 57–59, *58*
Deutsche Bank 19
Dewaele, Tom 105
Disney 100, 136
diversity 6, 17, 50, 139

empathy 17, 33–34, 37–39, 95–96, 117,
        122, 130, 132, 153, 161
employee experience, ecosystem
    approach 42–43, 50–52
    challenges 44
    8XP framework 53–60, *58*
    evolution 41–42
    EX understanding 52–53
    focus 44–45
    and HEX 45–48, *47–48*
    outcomes 48–50
employee journey 4–7, 8, 88, 102, 103, 105,
        150, 155–58, 160, 166, 169
    designs and practices 9–13
    employee experience, understanding of
        (case study) 139–44
    employee journey mapping 73
    EX teams, performance 77–79
    experience mindset 67–68
    holistic employee experience (HEX)
        model 44–45
    MAD milestones 128–32
    present moment performance 171–72
    see also employee experience, ecosystem;
        leadership, reinventing
employee value proposition (EVP) 66, 160
employees
    certain leadership 133–34
    co-creation, transformation 37–39
    communication 117
    EX technology 8
    EX understanding 52–53
    financial crisis 20–21

global pandemic 9–11
HR, role 169–71
insights 149–54
journey 4–7
leadership 95–96
MAD milestones 128–32
management ideas 1–3
micro management 125
pay scale 21–22
people strategy 16–19
strategy and roles 24–26
team performance, creating 81–88
time management 166–68
and uncertainty 19–20
workforces, expectations 22–24
see also co-creation; HEX performance
employer brand 85, 140, 142, 145, 160
employers 10, 11, 13, 17, 18, 136–37, 150
  financial crisis 20–21
  metaverse 70–72
  strategy and roles 24–26
  sustainability 137–44, *138*
  talent shortage 21–22
  time 166–68
  universal approach 42–43
  see also HEX performance
EX leaders 76, 136, 142, 144–45, 164
  articulating EX 30–31
  belonging 6–7
  brand 145–47
  brand leadership 164–65
  challenging and co-creating 165–66
  co-creation groups 29–30, *29*
  8XP framework 53–60, *58*
  EX understanding 52–53
  experience and performance 24–26
  high employee experience performance,
      planning 81–89
  holistic employee experience (HEX)
      model 44–45
  insights 149–59
  leadership, reinventing 109–19, *113,
      115, 118*
  LUCK 32–37
  management ideas 1–3
  people and human experience 159–61
  profile of 68
  role of 74
  team approach 80–81
  technology performance 97–99
  time 166–68
  workplace 9–13
EX playbook 30, 42, 143
EX strategy, winning

actions 144–45
brand 145–47
rusted and positive community 135–37
sustainability 137–44, *138*
EX teams 42, 53, 56, 68, 146, 150–51
  performance 77–79
  practitioners, mindset of 79–80
  team approach 80–81
  team performance, creating 81–88
EX workshop 29
EX, evaluations
  insights 149–54
  L'Oréal (case study) 154–59
  people and human experience 159–61
ExecOnline 108, 109
experience masterplan 63–66, *65*
  actions 69
  experience mindset 67–68
  focus on 73–74
  map 69–70
  mechanisms 73
  moments 74–76, *75*
  technology 70–72
  vision 66–67
ExpressVPN 72

feedback 38, 49, 64, 94, 116,
      140, 144, 171
  workplace performance 99–101
flexibility 9, 22, 92, 94, 123, 12, 156
Forbes 125
France 141
future of work 3, 100, 108, 166

Gartner 172
Glassdoor 18, 136, 170
global pandemic 9–11, 16, 24, 37, 71, 86,
      92, 152, 154, 167, 172
  technology performance 97–99
  and uncertainty 19–20
  see also HEX performance;
      workplace

Hastings, Reed 112
HEX performance 93–94
  community performance 101–03
  human performance 94–95
  leadership 95–96
  purpose and impact 103–04
  structural performance 97
  technology 97–99
  Unilever (case study) 104–05
  workplace performance 99–101
Hogan, Kathleen 37

holistic employee experience (HEX)
    model 44, 45–48, 47–48, 53, 59,
    73, 85, 114, 117–19, 118, 128, 141,
    165, 172
    see also leadership, reinventing
Houser, Dan 68
HR. See human resources (HR)
human capitalism 3
human resource director (HRD) 81
human resources (HR) 17, 23, 70, 96, 140,
    141–42, 155
    disruption of 3–4
    employee journey 4–7
    global pandemic 9–11
    HR strategy 50–52
    LUCK 32–37
    metaverse 70–72
    people and human experience 159–61
    people strategy 16–19
    positive relationships 133–34
    role 169–71
    talent rotation 7
    technology performance 97–99
    transformation of 150–51
    see also HEX performance

Iger, Bob 100, 136
inclusion 6, 50
information 33, 35–36, 38, 72, 99, 128,
    163, 169

Keats, John 138
Kierkegaard 26

L'Oréal 154–59
La Maison Sanofi 141
labour market 20, 24, 92
layoffs 45, 92, 96
leadership, reinventing
    alignment 109–10
    capabilities 110–11
    core capabilities 114–19, 115, 118
    quality 111–13, 113
learning and development (L&D) 17
Lever, William Hesketh 104
life bingo card 74–76, 75
lived experience 24–25, 26, 50, 60, 87, 110,
    121–22, 127, 139
Lyft 100

MA 141
management
    co-creation, requirements 31–37
    employee journey 4–7

focus 44–45
global pandemic 9–11
ideas 1–3
mindset 7
people strategy 16–19
strong strategy 19–20
managers 22–23, 37, 50, 80, 81, 107, 171
    aligning 151
    HEX leadership 117–18, 118
    leadership quality 111–13, 113
    MAD milestones 128–32
marketing 45–46, 53, 70, 81, 85, 128,
    142, 160
Meta 136, 167
Microsoft 23, 37
A Million Conversations (Sanofi) 143
Musk, Elon 112–13

Nadella, Satya 37
Netflix 100, 112
Nike 71

Office for National Statistics (ONS) 10, 22
OpenAI 172
opportunity 4, 9, 13, 21, 30, 44, 52, 59, 96,
    105, 127, 133, 142, 152, 160, 174
organization and planet (OP) framework 34
organizational culture 24–25, 30, 75, 104

Paris 141, 156
Peltz, Nelson 136
Pixley 109
Pixley, Sara 108
platforms 41, 46, 58–59, 83, 86, 87, 121,
    168, 170–71
    EX technology 8
    global technology platform 1
    leadership capabilities 110–11
    rating 18
    technology performance 97–99
Port Sunlight 104
PricewaterhouseCoopers survey 22

'quiet quitting' 2, 23–24, 109, 130, 132

Redmond, Eric 71
return on experience (RoE) 57, 92–93
Rockstar Games 68
Rumpler, Claude 155, 156

salaries 20, 128, 138
Sanofi 139–44
Schueller, Eugène 154–55
shareholders 159, 168, 174

Shopify 100, 167
skills 4, 5, 17, 31, 39, 46, 59, 68, 74,
        113, 161
    HR skills 141–42
    leadership capabilities 110–11
stakeholders 12, 28, 30, 37, 49, 108, 129,
        135, 161, 168, 173
    employee experience, understanding of
        (case study) 139–44

technology 10, 13, 27, 34, 35, 78, 88, 93,
        109, 144, 152, 172
    EX technology 8
    global technology platform 1
    HR model 3–4
    leadership capabilities 110–11
    metaverse 70–72
    outcomes 48–50
    technology performance 97–99
    workplace performance 99–101
Twilio 167
Twitter 112

UK workforce 10
Ukraine 20
Unilever 104–05
United Kingdom (UK) 22, 102, 104
United States of America (USA) 20, 72, 141

Venice 97
Verma, Raj 139, 140–42
virtual reality (VR) 70–71

Washington Post 109
workers 7, 10, 12, 44, 56, 66, 71, 100, 104,
        124, 172
    co-creation 29–30, 29
    human performance 94–95
    pandemic and 20, 92
    people and human experience 159–61
    progress 144–45
    talented workers 122
Workplace Intelligence 108
workplace
    area of 122–23
    co-creation, requirements 31–37
    coordinate and connect 123–25
    designs and practices 9–13
    employee experience, understanding of
        (case study) 139–44
    financial crisis 20–21
    L'Oréal (case study) 154–59
    MAD milestones 128–32
    metaverse 70–72
    pay scale 21–22
    people leaders, emergence 2–3
    people strategy 16–19
    performance 99–101
    positive relationships 133–34
    technology performance 97–99
    work and time 125–28
    workforces, expectations 22–24
World Economic Forum 143

'Your Voice' 140

Printed in the USA
CPSIA information can be obtained
at www.ICGtesting.com
LVHW070625080923
757540LV00015B/292

9 781398 608825